An Introduction
to the Study of Luke-Acts

Other titles in the T&T Clark Approaches to Biblical Studies series include:

An Introduction
to the Study of Luke-Acts

V. GEORGE SHILLINGTON

t&t clark

Published by T&T Clark
A Continuum imprint
The Tower Building, 11 York Road, London SE1 7NX
80 Maiden Lane, Suite 704, New York, NY 10038

www.tandtclark.com

First published 2007

Reprinted 2011

British Library Cataloguing-in-Publication Data
A catalogue record for this book is available from the British
Library.

ISBN-10: 0567030539 (paperback)
ISBN-13: 9780567030535 (paperback)

Typeset by Free Range Book Design & Production
Printed and bound in Great Britain

For
PHILIPPE AND MATHIEU;
LIAM AND LOGAN
adorable
grandsons

Contents

Acknowledgements

I owe a debt of gratitude to scholars of Luke-Acts whose labour lies behind much of the substance of the book. I regret that the format did not permit full notation of their work, apart from citation in the Bibliography and in 'Further reading' sections. A number of the persons listed will recognize *intertexture* traceable to their work.

I also wish to acknowledge the kind and competent assistance of the librarian, Vic Froese, at Canadian Mennonite University, for making my search for resources less tedious and time-consuming.

To my son Ralph, for offering himself as a sounding board via instant messaging for ideas I had along the way, a big thank you.

As I write this Acknowledgement, my other son, Brad, is serving in Afghanistan in an effort to improve the lot of the people in that country. I miss his stalwart friendship.

As always, my wife Grace is a constant source of encouragement and wisdom.

VGS
March 2006
Winnipeg

1

Luke-Acts: an aerial view

While this book presents some new insights from reading Luke-Acts alternatively, it does not pretend to do full justice to all the variegated texture of this lengthy two-part work. There are numerous commentaries of recent vintage that serve that purpose. The aim of this volume is twofold: (1) to apply different reading models to key texts in Luke-Acts, and (2) to capture, in the process, major interrelated features between these two important books of the New Testament from the pen of one writer.

How to use the book

The book is not a monograph for scholars of Luke-Acts, but a guide for students at the entry level to college or university. Therefore, it does not have footnotes, but does include a few embedded references to secondary sources. Nor is there argument between various scholarly positions on this or that point of exegesis. Readers can consult the sources listed under 'Further reading', and also in the Bibliography, to expand their horizon. The 'Review questions' should help focus the issues and aid in comprehension.

Scripture quotations are from the New Revised Standard Version (NRSV), unless otherwise indicated. It would help to read each of Luke and Acts at one sitting to become familiar with the literary and thematic landscape before engaging with the chapters of the book. While some texts are incorporated into the discussion, most are not. Thus, readers are strongly advised to have the Bible handy for checking references made throughout the discussion.

The name 'Luke' is used consistently throughout the book to refer to the 'Gospel according to Luke', not to the author of Luke-Acts. The historical author does not disclose her/his name in either of the documents. In keeping with the historical approach used in the first two chapters I refer to the one responsible for the two books as 'the author', elsewhere as the 'implied author', or the 'Lukan author'. In so doing, I have tried to respect the internal anonymity of the two-part work. (Note: 'narrator' should not be confused with 'author' or 'implied author'. The 'narrator' is a character internal to the text. See Chapter 6.)

Luke-Acts overview

An overview of a literary composition is no substitute for exploring the details of its multi-faceted texture. At the same time, an overview can help locate the basic features of a work, within which to understand the particulars of a given part thereof. It is much like having an aerial view of the city in which a person lives and moves.

Luke

The Prologue and Dedication (1.1-4)

A. The origin(s) of Jesus (1.5–2.52)
… including the angelic *announcement* to Zechariah of the unusual birth of the forerunner of Jesus, John the Baptist (1.5-25); the angelic *announcement* to Mary of the miraculous birth of Jesus by the power of the Holy Spirit (1.6-56); the *birth*, circumcision and description of John (1.59-80); the *birth*, circumcision and description of Jesus (2.1-40); Jesus at 12 in the Temple of Jerusalem (2.41-52).

B. Jesus getting ready for ministry (3.1–4.13)
… including the preaching and imprisonment of John the Baptist (3.1-20); the baptism, genealogy, and temptation of Jesus (3.21–4.13)

C. Jesus of Nazareth teaches, heals and calls disciples in Galilee (4.14–9.50)
… including a threat on his life at Nazareth (4.14-30); preaching, healing, and catching fish at Capernaum (4.31–5.16); controversies with the Pharisees (5.12–6.11); choosing the Twelve and the sermon on the plain (6.12-49); testimony about John the Baptist, judgement on this generation, parables (7.1–8.21); calming the storm, casting a demon from a man into pigs, bringing a young girl back to life; the mission of the Twelve (8.22–9.10); feeding the crowd, Peter's

confession, the passion foretold, the Transfiguration (9.11-36); more miracles and rivalry among the disciples (9.37-50).

C. The Lukan journey of Jesus to Jerusalem (9.51–18.14)

... including an incident with some Samaritans (9.51-62); mission of the Seventy [-two] (10.1-20); parable of the Good Samaritan (10.21-37); Mary and Martha (10.38-42); prayer and the Lord's Prayer (11.1-13); opposition/accusation about Beelzebul (11.14-26); the sign of Jonah, Holy Spirit, and various sayings (11.29–12.15); parable of the rich fool and related sayings (12.16–13.9); healing a crippled woman on the Sabbath, parables, reception/rejection of the kingdom (13.10-30); Herod's desire to kill Jesus, and Lament over Jerusalem (13.31-5); a healing, sayings/parables of a great dinner, salt, lost sheep, lost coin, prodigal son, dishonest manager (14.1–16.15); the law, divorce, parable of the rich man and Lazarus, stumbling-blocks, forgiveness, faith, unprofitable servants (16.16–17.10); cleansing ten lepers, God's kingdom coming, Son of Man, parables of dishonest judge and Pharisee and tax collector (17.11–18.14). [At this point Luke connects somewhat with Mark.] Jesus blesses little children, talks to a rich young man and disciples about riches (18.15-30); announcement of the passion, healing a blind man at Jericho, Zacchaeus meets Jesus (18.31–19.10); parable of the pounds (19.11-27).

D. Jesus in Jerusalem (19.28–21.38)

... including regal entry into the city and Temple (19.28-40); lament over Jerusalem and clearing the Temple (19.41-6); reaction of Jewish leaders, Jesus' authority in dispute (19.47–20.8); parable of the wicked tenants, paying tribute, resurrection of the dead, Son of David (20.9-44); the scribes, the widow's tiny offering, the fate of the Temple, signs of the end of the age (20.45–21.11); prepare for persecution, the coming of the Son of Man, vigilance (21.11-38).

E. Narrative of Jesus' suffering and death (22.1–23.56)

... including conspiracy (22.1-2); betrayal (22.3-6); last supper (Passover) (22.7-23); disciples and their roles, Peter's denial coming, two swords (22.24-38); prayer on Mount of Olives, arrest, Peter's denial (22.39-71); Jesus tried before Pilate, then Herod, the sentence of death by crucifixion (23.1-25); carrying the cross, crucifixion, the two criminals, the death and burial of Jesus (23.26-56)

F. The narrative of Jesus' resurrection/ascension (24.1-53)

... including women at the empty tomb (24.1-12); appearance on the road to Emmaus (24.13-35); appearance to disciples in Jerusalem (24.36-43); commission (24.44-9); ascension (24.50-3).

Acts

Prologue and repeated dedication (1.1-2)

A. The primitive community of Jesus in Jerusalem (1.3-26)

... including Jesus' last words, commission, ascension (1.3-11); meeting to choose a replacement for Judas (1.12-26).

B. The mission of Peter as representative of the Twelve in Jerusalem/Judaea (2.1–8.4)

... including Pentecost and the poured-out Spirit (2.1-13); Peter's sermon to Israel, responses, life together (2.14-47); Peter heals a cripple at the Temple, preaches there (3.1-26); Peter and John in Jerusalem court, prayer, persecution, a common-purse community, apostles persecuted (4.1–5.42).

C. The seven Hellenistai leaders (6.1–8.40)

... including choosing of the Seven for administrative ministry (6.1-7); Stephen's speech and stoning to death with Paul's approval (6.8–8.1a); persecution of the *Hellenistai* (8.1b-4); Philip preaches in Samaria, baptizes an Ethiopian on the road to Gaza (8.5-40).

D. Paul the persecutor transformed into Paul the missionary for Jesus (9.1-31)

E. Peter's understanding of Jewish association with Gentiles transformed (9.32–11.18)

F. The word spreads to Greeks with the scattering of the Hellenistai (11.19–12.25)

... including the preaching of Barnabas at Antioch (11.19-26); a collection of money from Antioch to Jerusalem, persecution of James and Peter, Herod's death (11.27–12.25).

G. Mission narrative about Paul and Barnabas among Jews and Gentiles in Asia (13.1–14.28)

... including preaching in Cyprus (13.1-12); Pisidian Antioch (13.13-52); Iconium (14.1-7); Lystra and Derbe (14.8-20); and return/report to Antioch (14.21-8).

H. The Jerusalem conference about the mission to Gentiles (15.1-35)

... including the question about circumcising believing Gentiles (15.1-2); Peter's appeal in favour of including them (15.3-12); James' support of Peter's argument and a proposal (15.13-21); the letter to Gentile communities stating the requirement for Gentiles (15.22-35).

I. Paul's other missionary travels and experiences (15.36–21.16)

... including Paul's separation from Barnabas and choice of Silas as partner (15.36-40); circumcision of Timothy at Lystra/Derbe (15.41-16.5); preaching and healing across Asia (16.6-10); crossing to Philippi (16.11-40); then Thessalonica and Berea (17.1-15); the Areopagus at Athens (17.16-34); Corinth (18.1-17); return to Antioch (18.18-22); Paul returns to Ephesus, finds friends of Apollos and disciples of John, preaches, witnesses a riot (18.23–19.41); leaves Macedonia, Achaia and Syria (20.1-6); stops at Troas, then Miletus to say farewell to leaders from Ephesus (20.7-38); returns to Jerusalem (21.1-16).

J. Paul's arrest and trial in Jerusalem and appeal to Caesar (21.17–26.32)

... including visits with James and the elders (21.17-25); arrest (21.26-40); speech to the crowd in Jerusalem (22.1-21); imprisonment and trial continue in Caesarea and Jerusalem with Paul giving testimony before the Jewish Council, Governors Felix, Festus and Herod Agrippa, Paul appeals to Caesar (22.22–26.32)

K. Paul goes to Rome and remains under house arrest for two years (27.1–28.31)

... including storm and shipwreck (27.1-44); a winter stay at Malta (28.1-10); arrival and arrest in Rome (28.11-16); speaks openly about Jesus to important Jewish people (28.17-29); lives under arrest at his own expense and welcomes all who come to him (28.30-1).

Further reading

A very accessible introduction to the various approaches used throughout this book is that of Steve Moyise, *Introduction to Biblical Studies*, 2nd edn (2004). See also my *Reading the Sacred Text* (2002), pp. 206–96.

2

Historical enquiry: composition, context and intention

There are two ways of reading a document that purports to give worthwhile historical information. One is to read for facts of history *narrated within* the document, and the other is to enquire into the factors *involved in writing* the document. Results of the second way of reading facilitate the understanding of the first way of reading. In other words, the more a reader knows about the composition of a document the more light is shed on the material internal to the document.

This is abundantly so in the interpretation of Luke-Acts. Both the Gospel of Luke and the Acts of the Apostles are loaded with clues about the character, circumstances, purpose and thought patterns of the writer. These all play a part in the transmission of the material (persons, events, speeches, motives, etc.) encoded in the narratives of Luke-Acts. Moreover, this chapter will attempt to set forth factors involved in the writing of Luke-Acts, before investigating historical elements narrated within the two-part document in the next chapter.

A critical realist approach

How does one tackle the reading of Luke-Acts in this twofold way, with historical understanding? The answer resides, not within Luke-Acts and related literature, but within the conscious thinking of the reader. I am proposing a critical realist approach in this chapter and the next. A critical realist approach stands over against a naive realist approach. A naive realist claims to take things at face value, to perceive 'the world' that is simply out there, and to know its reality without question. No need, for example, to investigate the table on which my computer rests while I write. A table is a table. But it turns out this table has no legs. Is it really 'a table'?

In the reading of Luke-Acts, the operation will not happen automatically or unconsciously. The exercise will involve first, *experiencing* the data of texts in Luke-Acts; second, *understanding* what we experience there; third, *judging* the viability and value of what we experience and understand, and fourth, *deciding/acting* on the judgement made. This whole operation happens dynamically, spontaneously. The final stage – deciding/acting – in the reading operation can be articulated across a spectrum of possibility, probability or certainty.

The key to a critical realist approach to Luke-Acts is the reader's self-appropriation of these four stages of knowing. Of course, human experience is necessarily value-laden. We bring to our reading the dynamic store of insights that make our life meaningful. But insights are always subject to revision in light of new evidence. Critical realism is at the heart of what is generally referred to as historical-critical interpretation in biblical studies. It asks seriously and honestly: What is really going on in the texture of this text? What was really moving forward in the particular history represented in the text?

Faith communities are often suspicious of the historical-critical approach to reading biblical texts. They fear the approach will erode the fabric of faith and faithfulness. While that may indeed happen in some cases, a grasp of historical truth, towards which a critical realist approach strives, should strengthen faith, not destroy it. Truth in any sphere should accomplish that goal. It may mean revision and adjustment in faith-understanding, but not abandonment of faith. With these few qualifiers in place, we may proceed with an historical enquiry into Luke-Acts from the vantage point of its composition.

Redactor and author

One of the principal questions the historical-critical approach poses is this: Who wrote Luke-Acts? Finding an answer to that question is a bit like 'Finding Forrester'. The question is not answered merely by putting a name to the writer, but by finding out about the character of the person whose composition captures our imagination: his aims and interests and intention in writing this work of biblical literature.

In the case of Luke-Acts, as compared, say, to the letters of Paul, the designation 'redactor' may be more to the point than 'author'. A redactor works with sources in bringing the volume to its final form. But the sources are not simply strung together at random. They are incorporated meaningfully, modified if necessary, made to fit the plan and purpose of the overall project. An 'author', such a Paul, proceeds to write out of his head and heart with purpose and persuasion. Yet in a very real sense the redactor of Luke-Acts is also author. He uses sources, probably both oral and written, purposefully to accomplish some end in his readers' mind and life. When scholars look for the 'redaction' woven into the tapestry of Luke-Acts, they are trying to identify the elements beyond the source material that bespeak the author's interests and emphases.

But the identity of the historical figure responsible for the composition continues to fascinate many scholars. Tradition, going back to the second century, has identified Luke 'the beloved physician', friend of Paul, a Gentile, as the author of both Luke and Acts (Col. 4.14; Phlm. 24; 2 Tim. 4.11). His name as author appears first in the Muratorian Canon of the late second century, and his role as author of both volumes is argued in Irenaeus (*ca.* 180). Origen in the third century thought 'Luke' meant 'Lucius' of Romans 16.21, a relative of Paul. Others thought 'Luke' was Lucius of Cyrene in Acts 13.1, one of the leaders of the church at Antioch. In the end, the earlier tradition of Luke 'the beloved physician' as author gained a firm hold in the Church down to the present time.

By the end of the second century it had become important for the Church to identify Christian writings with Apostles. If the writer was not an Apostle, then he should be someone closely allied with an Apostle. From the so-called 'we' passages of Acts (16.8-17; 20.5-15; 21.1-18; 27.1–28.16), scholars since Irenaeus have assumed that the writer of these first-person plural narratives must have accompanied Paul on the occasions noted in the passages. The 'we' may have come from a personal travel diary. Hence the appearance of 'we' in the respective narratives. Luke, the beloved physician of Colossians 4.14, would be as good a candidate as any. The Greek of Luke-Acts is that of an educated man, and the special interest in medicine in both Luke and Acts suggests a physician as author (e.g. Luke 4.38; 5.12; 8.44; Acts 5.5, 10; 9.40; 12.23).

But this traditional identity of the author of Luke-Acts does not rest on an unshakeable foundation. Luke-Acts does not show any more interest in medicine than many other writings of educated people of the time. Nor is the medical language any more technical than that of the Greek Scriptures of Judaism (LXX), in which the author is evidently immersed. As for the 'we' passages, they prove nothing more than possibly (1) the product of an eyewitness, not necessarily the author, and (2) an inclusive way of writing, found in the author's source and retained in his narrative.

More telling still is the relation between Paul of Acts and Paul of the Letters. There is no evidence in Acts that the author was familiar with the Letters of Paul. Or if he was familiar with them he chose to ignore them as sources for Paul's thought and mission. Acts depicts Paul as a protégé of Gamaliel of Jerusalem, having spent his youth in that city (Acts 22.3). Paul admits no such situation, even when it would have served his purpose to do so. Paul in the Letters recounts being in Jerusalem only once before the Apostolic Conference, and then once after that with the Collection, for a total of three times following his conversion (Gal. 1.15-24; 2.1-10; Rom. 15.25-6). Acts, on the other hand, reports five journeys to Jerusalem (Acts chs 9, 11, 15, 18.22 and 21).

Paul's apostolic status was important to him, according to the Letters. Not so in Acts. The group of the Twelve (which does not include Paul) is prominent in both Luke and Acts. Only once does the author use the title 'Apostle' for Paul, and that insignificantly along with Barnabas (Acts 14.14). This is strange indeed if the author was a friend and colleague who knew the struggles Paul went through to maintain his apostleship (e.g. 2 Cor. 11.15; Gal. 1.1-19).

The difference between the two 'Pauls' is marked more by the difference between the two patterns of thought. Paul of Acts makes mission speeches that scarcely touch the major issues that so occupy Paul in the Letters. Paul's Areopagus speech (Acts 17) to the philosophers of Athens, for example, highlights the oneness of God and of all humanity – classic Jewish doctrine – by citing two Greek poets, something Paul is not wont to do in his Letters. Furthermore, the centrality of the death of Jesus by crucifixion for the sake of humanity is absent altogether (cf. 1 Cor. 1.22-4). The resurrection, instead, is uppermost in the Areopagus speech, a doctrine close to the heart of the redactor of Acts. Of course, there is always the conjecture that Luke, friend of Paul, selected only what he wanted from the Letters and from memory in keeping with his own inclination in his writing.

In the end, the identity of the author of Luke-Acts by a name external to the writing is not so important. More important for the interpretation of the two volumes is the identification of the character and purpose of the author as found in Luke-Acts itself. And to that concern we now attend.

Upon examination of the text of Luke-Acts, we discover several salient features that play into the interpretation of the work. Discussion of these features falls under a few leading questions.

1. Was the author an educated person with an interest in writing a history of the Christian Church?

The prologue to Luke (1.1-4) is among the finest Greek literary constructions in the New Testament, taking its place alongside the prologue to Hebrews. Such a prologue was characteristic of important treatises in the Greek literary world. While the author does not give his name, he does present his aim and procedure in writing, from which we can infer something of his character. First, he follows others who have written an 'orderly account' (*diegesis*) of the events. Second, his work leading up to the writing of his own 'orderly account' was thorough, 'after investigating everything from the very first'. Third, he dedicates his literary product to 'most excellent Theophilus'. Here is an author (a man presumably) who knows the art of introducing a literary work, recognizes the cognate work of others, establishes his own contribution as worthy of respect, and then dedicates the work to someone significant, perhaps a patron of the art.

There can be little doubt that Luke-Acts exhibits the marks of historical writing of the time, not unlike that of his Jewish contemporary, Josephus. That does not mean that he was writing history for the sake of history. Rather, he was writing history for the purpose of proclamation and persuasion. In his own words, he was writing so that Theophilus – and others like him – 'may know the truth concerning the things about which you have been instructed' (1.4).

2. Was the author Gentile or Jewish?

The answer depends on whether the author was Luke the physician or someone else. If Luke the physician, then he was Gentile. Paul excludes Luke from 'the only ones of the circumcision among [his] co-workers' (Col. 4.11, 14). Luke-Acts does show a real interest in the mission to the Gentiles from beginning to end, from the prophetic oracle of Simeon in the Temple of Jerusalem (Luke 2.29-32) to Paul's final preaching in Rome (Acts 28.28-31). Yet this explicit interest in the Gentiles does not make the author Gentile. Paul was profoundly interested in the mission to the Gentiles, yet he was Jewish. It is quite likely that the author lives and breathes the Pauline tradition that bristles with echoes and allusions to the successful mission to the Gentiles. The author is also interested in Samaritans (Luke 10.30-6; 9.52-7; 17.11-16; Acts 1.8; 8.1ff), but that does not make him Samaritan.

I rather think the author was a Hellenistic Jewish man, not unlike Stephen, but not Palestinian. An intimate knowledge of the province of Palestine is lacking in his work. But his knowledge of the Jewish Scriptures and Jewish tradition is second to none. John Drury's argument to this effect is thoroughly convincing. Drury sees in the author's copious citations and echoes of the Jewish faith tradition, especially that of the Greek Scriptures of Hellenistic Judaism, compelling evidence of the Jewish background and character of the author of Luke-Acts. Stephen's speech, as much a creation by the author as of Stephen, captures the story of Israel from Abraham to

Solomon with native authority (Acts 7.2-51). A Gentile, even an educated one, could hardly be expected to display such gifted Jewishness. But the author is also Hellenistic. His Greek literary skill is that of a person immersed in a Hellenistic environment, not unlike the person of Philo, a Jewish philosopher of Alexandria in Egypt.

3. Was the author pro-Jewish or pro-Roman?

Having proposed that the author of Luke-Acts was more likely Jewish than Gentile, it should follow that his composition would be pro-Jewish. But that is not the case. A case can be made for this author, as for other disenfranchised Jews, that his Jewish-Christian stance informs his anti-Jewish posturing in Luke-Acts. The same holds for the Jewish community at Qumran. They had little good to say about their fellow Jews in Jerusalem. Similarly, Paul, being Jewish, can criticize his fellow Jews when they take position against him (e.g. 2 Cor. 11.19-25; 1 Thess. 2.14-16). The Jews in Luke-Acts were regularly the culprits creating trouble for the early believers in Jesus Messiah. Their persecution of Paul in Damascus – Gentile territory! – is a case in point (Acts 9.24-7; *contra* 2 Cor. 11.32-3).

Luke-Acts hesitates to cast aspersion on the Romans. The motive is not obvious. Possibly the author is trying to gain the respect of the Roman authorities for the benefit of the Church in the same way the Jews had done for their synagogues. Paul is regularly protected by Roman leaders (Acts 23.23ff; 24.22ff; 25.14ff), and given safe passage to Rome after his trial in Jerusalem (Acts 27.1ff). When in Rome, Paul is allowed to meet with people and preach the good news of the kingdom of God freely. Readers are left wondering at the end of Acts if the trial in Rome ever happened. Or if it did happen, was Paul exonerated or executed? In any case, the author is not prepared to cast the Roman authorities in a bad light, and certainly not as the executioners of the dominant hero of the narrative (*diegesis*) of Acts.

Implied time, place and situation in life

Equally important for the interpretation of a literary work such as Luke-Acts is the time and setting of the composition. Was it written during Paul's imprisonment in Rome while the issues of the mission were still fresh in everyone's mind? (For example the issue of Paul's view of the role of the Law in the conversion of the Gentiles?) Was it written while the Temple of Jerusalem was still in full swing? Or were Jerusalem and the Temple only a memory after the destruction by Titus in 70 CE? Was it written in Palestine or beyond that province? What was the situation in the life of the author's church that might have given rise to the two volumes?

Answers to these questions do not come easily. Nor is there agreement on the date and provenance of the composition of Luke-Acts.

An early date of the late sixties, before the outcome of the trial of Paul in Rome, has had supporters to this day. Others have placed the time of writing in the early second century, presuming that the author of Luke-Acts was dependent on the work of Josephus, published at the end of the first century. Neither of these extremes fits the facts.

By the author's own admission in the prologue to Luke, 'many have undertaken to set down an orderly account of the events that have been fulfilled among us' (1.1). Gospels were not in circulation by the end of the sixties. Mark may have come to the fore by the end of that decade, but not 'many', and certainly not Luke-Acts. The author of Luke-Acts appears to rely on Mark among other sources for the production of his own work. Such a situation demands a time-frame of at least five years for the earlier Gospels to become known throughout the Christian communities in the Mediterranean basin. That in itself puts the composition and publication of Luke-Acts no earlier than 75 CE.

The prologue to Luke further militates against the early date on another point. The author recognizes the transmission of the traditions through two generations of transmitters down to his own: 'they were handed on to us by those who from the beginning were (1) eyewitnesses and (2) servants of the word' (1.2). From this we may infer that the eyewitnesses, namely the Apostles, had died, and likewise the servants of the word. This situation would put the writing of Luke-Acts no earlier than 75 CE, and more probably 85 CE.

The author keeps his eye explicitly on the *narrative* time of his work, which is from Jesus to Paul, so we should not expect to find explicit reference to the destruction of the Temple and Jerusalem in 70 CE in Luke or Acts. But echoes of the destruction come through loudly in Luke at the point of Jesus' prediction of the destruction of the Temple. Compared to Mark's rendering of Jesus' prediction, with its apocalyptic expansion (13.1-37), Luke's apocalypse reverberates with the events of destruction already in memory (21.5-28) (See Fig. 2.1). It describes what happened when the Roman General Titus ravaged the Temple and city with a vengeance, causing inhabitants to flee to the mountains, prohibiting the people to re-enter.

Mark 13.1-37	Luke 21.5-28
As he came out of the temple, one of his disciples said to him, 'Look, Teacher, what large stones and what large buildings!' Then Jesus asked him, 'Do you see these great buildings? Not one stone will be left here upon another; all will be thrown down.'	When some were speaking about the temple, how it was adorned with beautiful stones and gifts dedicated to God, he said, 'As for these things that you see, the days will come when not one stone will be left upon another; all will be thrown down.'
[This is followed by an apocalyptic expansion of the prediction, *without further mention of Jerusalem or the Temple*.]	[This is followed by an apocalyptic expansion, *with further mention of Jerusalem as follows:*]
	'When you see Jerusalem surrounded by armies, then know that its desolation has come near. Then those in Judaea must flee to the mountains, and those inside the city must leave it, and those out in the country must not enter it; for these are days of vengeance, as a fulfilment of all that is written.'

Figure 2.1

Moreover, the time-setting of the composition of Luke is between 75 and 85, and the composition of Acts some time after that, perhaps 85–90 CE.

As for the place of origin of Luke-Acts, a number of centres have been proposed: Antioch, Rome, Ephesus, Macedonia, Achaia, or some centre in Asia Minor. Not very helpful!

I think it is safe to say that the author wrote his two volumes from one of the locations mentioned in Acts. But which one? There are so many. Alexandria could be entered into the list noted above, and Apollos cited as the author (Acts 19.24-8). After all, this Apollos was eloquent, 'well versed in the Scriptures', and 'taught accurately the things concerning Jesus' (cf. Luke 1.1-4). Yet I think Alexandria must come in a close second for the provenance of Luke-Acts.

A better case can be made for a centre in Macedonia, perhaps Philippi or Thessalonica, primarily because the author is familiar with terms and titles known and used locally. Acts describes Philippi correctly as a 'Roman colony' whose rulers are called *Strategoi* ('magistrates' NRSV). This title for city rulers is rarely found in a literary source, but it appears on inscriptions as a colloquial term used strictly in Philippi (Acts 16.12, 20-2). Similarly, the rulers of Thessalonica are called *Politarchai* (Acts 17.8, 'city officials' NRSV). Nowhere in Greek or

Latin literature is this term used of city officials. But archaeological discoveries have shown that local Thessalonian inhabitants used the term for their city rulers.

For an author to be familiar with such local, colloquial designations argues for the origin of the document from that location: the area of Macedonia in which Philippi and Thessalonica are located.

Another tentative point may be made about the author's setting-in-life given this location in Macedonia. Paul depicts the Macedonian believers in Jesus as abundantly generous in the midst of poverty; joyful in the face of ordeal. Paul applauds the Macedonians for their overflowing fellowship in his ministry (2 Cor. 8.1-5). Both Luke and Acts wrestle with these very issues of poverty and fellowship and the Spirit of Jesus. In Luke the poor are the blessed ones; they attain the kingdom of God (6.20). 'The poor, the crippled, the blind, and the lame' enjoy the parabolic dinner, while the rich are excluded (14.15-24). In Acts also the ideal community has divested itself of property for the sake of every member in the group. 'There was not a needy person among them' (Acts 4.32-7). All this corresponds rather well with the picture Paul paints in 2 Corinthians 8 of the Macedonian believers.

I am therefore inclined to think that Luke-Acts originated from such a faith-heritage as this Macedonian setting. Perhaps the author of Luke-Acts, living and writing 40 years after Paul, implicitly bemoans the fact that this earlier attitude of generosity in the fifties (Paul's mission) has dissipated: some members of his community are now rich and not sharing according to the Spirit of Jesus in the Gospel.

The question of sources

As mentioned above, the author admits using sources for his narrative (Luke 1.1-4). But, unlike a modern writer of history, this author does not identify his sources in a bibliography, much less in footnotes. A modern interpreter, then, is driven to peruse the texture of the author's texts to discover the sources embedded within the narrative. The point in such an enquiry is historical. If sources can be identified that pre-date the composition of Luke-Acts, then the interpreter can learn something of the self-definition of the community, or person, responsible for that earlier source. By thus discerning the self-definition of the source-community, reasonable attempts can then be made to show development of thought from the source setting-in-life to the redaction setting-in-life.

'Sources' usually refer to written documents behind the extant document. But some recent authors, Gerd Lüdemann in particular, speak of the 'character of the tradition', mainly because the specific parameters of a given source are difficult to mark out with certainty, especially so in Acts.

What are the sources, or traditions, of Luke-Acts? The answer for Luke can be stated more confidently than for Acts. The reason is that Luke can be compared with the other Gospels, canonical and extra-canonical, whereas Acts stands very much alone as a genre. The identification of 'sources' in Acts is more an educated guess than a disciplined comparative study.

For the Gospel of Luke it is reasonably safe to say that the author relied on Mark, although less so than Matthew did. The *sequence* of events in Luke 1.1–22.53 is essentially the sequence of Mark – even though Luke has only about seven-tenths of the *material* of Mark. Yet the author of Luke is not bound slavishly to Mark's sequence. Mark 6.1-6 (the rejection of Jesus at Nazareth) is moved forward in Luke (4.16-30); Mark 1.16-20 (Jesus' call of the first disciples) is moved back (5.1-11); the sequence of Mark 3.7-12 (a large crowd by the Sea of Galilee) followed by Mark 3.13-19 (Jesus appointing the Twelve) is reversed in Luke (6.12-19); and Mark 3.31-5 (the true family of Jesus) is moved back in Luke (8.19-20). Of course, the author of Luke interrupts the sequence at points to insert other material pertinent to his purpose, most significantly a large block of Lukan material set in a circuitous 'travel narrative' of Jesus *en route* to Jerusalem (Luke 9.51–19.27). Similarly, Luke's birth, infancy and genealogy narratives (1.5–3.38) are the work of the Luke-Acts redactor quite apart from Mark. Finally, Luke's passion narrative (22.54–23.49) exhibits limited reliance on Mark's passion.

Another source that can be identified in Luke by comparison with Matthew is generally called 'Q' (for the German *Quelle* = source). The so-called Q material in Luke is not in the same sequence in Luke as in Matthew. Nor is the language of Q identical between Matthew and Luke, a situation that lends itself to some debate as to 'original Q'. Most scholars hold that a written source, rather than oral tradition, lies behind the Q material, and that the Q material is older than Mark. While Luke does not have all the material (mostly sayings) in the same sequence as Matthew, there are enough instances of sequence and similarity of language to warrant the conclusion that a written source funds this material in both Luke and Matthew. Figure 2.2 illustrates how Q material is configured in Matthew as compared to Luke.

Matthew	Luke
6.9-13: Our Father in heaven, hallowed be your name. Your kingdom come. Your will be done, on earth as it is in heaven. Give us this day our daily bread. And forgive us our debts, as we also have forgiven our debtors. And do not bring us to the time of trial, but rescue us from the evil one.	11.2-4: Father, hallowed be your name. Your kingdom come. Give us each day our daily bread. And forgive us our sins, for we ourselves forgive everyone indebted to us. And do not bring us to the time of trial.
5.3: Blessed are the poor in spirit, for theirs is the kingdom of heaven.	6.20: Blessed are you who are poor, for yours is the kingdom of God.
5.6: Blessed are those who hunger and thirst for righteousness, for they will be filled.	6.21: Blessed are you who are hungry now, for you will be filled.
8.19-20: A scribe then approached and said, 'Teacher, I will follow you wherever you go.' And Jesus said to him, 'Foxes have holes, and birds of the air have nests; but the Son of Man has nowhere to lay his head.'	9.57-60: As they were going along the road, someone said to him, 'I will follow you wherever you go.' And Jesus said to him, 'Foxes have holes, and birds of the air have nests; but the Son of Man has nowhere to lay his head.'
12.38-42: Then some of the scribes and Pharisees said to him, 'Teacher, we wish to see a sign from you.' But he answered them, 'An evil and adulterous generation asks for a sign, but no sign will be given to it except the sign of the prophet Jonah. For just as Jonah was three days and three nights in the belly of the sea monster, so for three days and three nights the Son of Man will be in the heart of the earth. The people of Nineveh will rise up at the judgement with this generation and condemn it, because they repented at the proclamation of Jonah, and see, something greater than Jonah is here! The queen of the South will rise up at the judgement with this generation and condemn it, because she came from the ends of the earth to listen to the wisdom of Solomon, and see, something greater than Solomon is here!	11.29-32: When the crowds were increasing, he began to say, 'This generation is an evil generation; it asks for a sign, but no sign will be given to it except the sign of Jonah. For just as Jonah became a sign to the people of Nineveh, so the Son of Man will be to this generation. The queen of the South will rise at the judgement with the people of this generation and condemn them, because she came from the ends of the earth to listen to the wisdom of Solomon, and see, something greater than Solomon is here!

Figure 2.2: Q in Matthew and Luke

As indicated already, the author of Luke-Acts had sources for Luke, whether oral or written, that were distinctly his own among the Gospel writers. The letter 'L' is applied to that material that cannot be assigned to Mark or Q. And the extent of that special material is significant. The opening of Luke (chs 1–3 – the origin of John the Baptist and Jesus) is peculiar to Luke, as is also the large travel narrative in chapters 9.51–18.14. In this latter section we have some of the most beloved parables, including the Good Samaritan and the Prodigal Son. Some scholars believe that Luke went through at least two stages of composition: (1) proto-Luke, which had the opening – without the classic Prologue (1.1-4) – and the special travel section (9.51–18.14), together with the passion narrative; this proto-Luke was circulated first; (2) Mark's sequence was then added, together with the Q material; the prologue made it ready for final publication. This composition sequence is nothing more than conjecture. There is good reason, rather, to treat the Gospel of Luke as it stands in the New Testament as an original publication, after some time investigating and incorporating sources, which can now be identified within the Gospel.

The sources for Acts are a very different matter. There can be no doubt that the author employed sources. Their identity, however, is at best tentative. If Paul's collected letters were not a primary source, as seems to be the case, then how does one identify the sources for Acts? Perhaps Gerd Lüdemann's proposal is sufficient: that the author of Acts used traditions (written and oral) from the Pauline mission territories. But this hardly accounts for the early chapters of Acts that deal with events and persons around Jerusalem, prior to Paul's mission.

About a century ago, Adolf von Harnack believed a Jerusalem-Caesarean source underwrites Acts 2–5, and an Antiochan source Acts 6–15. For the rest of Acts, chapter 16 to the end, the author would have found various traditions in the Pauline mission centres, including the travel diary format implicit in the 'we' passages (16.8-17; 20.5-15; 21.1-18; 27.1–28.16).

The speeches in Acts present a rather different scenario. Like other ancient writers of history, the author of Acts intersperses the narrative with key speeches given by significant characters in the unfolding drama. Each speech comes in at a strategic juncture. Peter's speeches in the early part of Acts represent the perspective of Jerusalem believers in Jesus (Acts 2), whereas Stephen's speech captures the sentiment of Hellenistic Jewish believers (Acts 7), and Paul's that of the message to the Gentiles (e.g. Acts 17). But where do these speeches come from? There was no recording device, and almost certainly no stenographer on hand at every moment to copy them. To suggest that the speakers wrote their speeches out in full in preparation for delivery, and that the author of Acts retrieved them years later, is very far-fetched.

More likely than not, the author, seeking to represent the various stages in the development of the Christian movement, created the speeches accordingly. What is remarkable is that every speech bears the literary and theological mark of the redactor of Acts. The speech of Stephen is somewhat more distinctive, but even there the author's hand is evident.

One question remains: What is the relevance of all of this historical investigation for the interpretation of Luke-Acts? If the above analysis is correct, we have an author using various sources to write a two-volume work about Jesus and the Church towards the end of the first century, some 40 years after Paul's mission, 20 years after the destruction of the Temple of Jerusalem by the Romans, from a place in northern Macedonia, when the Church experienced criticism from Judaism and pressure from the greater power of Rome. The end of the age had not come, and Jesus of Nazareth was no longer present in the Christ-community in the world. How do these factors shape the pattern of thought in Luke-Acts?

Premier emphases and conclusion

Suffice it to say that Luke-Acts exhibits distinctive patterns, or emphases, that reflect the situation outlined above.

1. The resurrected Jesus was '*taken up* to heaven' (Luke 24.50-3; Acts 1.2, 11, 22). Thus exalted, Jesus became Lord of the Church in the world.
2. The exalted Lord 'poured out' his Spirit to empower the Church for its ongoing life and mission in the world in the absence of Jesus (Acts 1.8; 2.1-13).
3. The outpoured Spirit in the community of faith is the same Spirit that came upon Mary at conception, and rested on Jesus during his earthly life and ministry (Luke 3.16-22).
4. The Spirit in the life of Jesus pleaded the cause of the despised of society, over against the rich and powerful: (a) sinners (Luke 5.1, 8; 7.36ff; 15.1ff; 18.9ff; 19.1ff); (b) shepherds (Luke 2.8-20); (c) Samaritans (Luke 10.30ff;17.11ff; cf. Acts 1.8; 8.1-14; 9.31); (d) women (Luke 7.12, 15; 8.2ff; 10.38ff; 23.27ff); (e) the destitute-poor (Luke 6.20; cf. 12.15ff; 16.19ff). The same Spirit should continue to energize the Church (Acts 2).
5. If the Church lives in the presence and power of the Spirit, Roman authorities will recognize its innocence (cf. Luke 23.47) and its value within the empire (Acts 23–28).

In short, this chapter has attempted to put Luke-Acts in its place. Without such an effort the reading of the historical, literary and theological elements internal to the narrative lack authentic context. An author's location in time and place and situation is bound to shape the literary outcome. That is true of modern, critical authors. How much more so of ancient, less critical authors!

At the same time, the reconstruction of an ancient author's context for the writing of his literary work is not absolute. The author of Luke-Acts has kept himself very much in the background of his work, pointing only to his diligence and purpose in bringing the work to the public forum under the auspices of the 'most excellent Theophilus' (Luke 1.4; Acts 1.1). The next chapter carries forward the project by investigating the value of the historical allusions the author makes within the narratives.

Further reading

The following go into more detail in some areas touched upon in this chapter: Werner Georg Kümmel, *Introduction to the New Testament* (1975), pp. 122–88; John Drane, *Introducing the New Testament* (2001), pp. 200–8, 237–65; John Drury, *Tradition and Design in Luke's Gospel* (1976); Robert M. Grant, *A Historical Introduction to the New Testament* (1963), pp. 74–91, 133–47; Jacob Jervell, *The Unknown Paul* (1984), pp. 68–76; Gerd Lüdemann, *Early Christianity according to the Traditions in Acts* (1989), pp. 1–18; Joel B. Green, *The Gospel of Luke* (1997), pp. 1–25; Ben Witherington III, *The Acts of the Apostles* (1998), pp. 1–102.

Review questions

1. Define/describe a 'critical realist' approach to reading Luke-Acts.
2. How does the term 'redaction' apply to Luke-Acts as compared to the Letters of Paul?
3. Why is the identity of the character and purpose of the 'author' more relevant than the identity of his name?
4. In what sense does the Areopagus speech (Acts 17) reflect more the theology of Luke-Acts than the theology of Paul in his Letters?
5. When and where was Luke-Acts written? How does this help in the reading of the two volumes?
6. How far is it possible to detect sources for Luke on the one hand and Acts on the other?

7. To what extent is the historical enquiry into the composition of
    Luke-Acts relevant to its interpretation?

3

Historical enquiry: events and people inside the text

Luke-Acts sets itself up for enquiry into its historical allusions integrated into its 'orderly narrative' (Luke 1.1-4). Of all four canonical Gospels, Luke stands out as the one most committed to setting the person and work of Jesus squarely within the historical facts and features of a particular time and place. Acts singularly distinguishes itself among the documents of the New Testament as the one to trace the development of the Christian Church from Easter to the imprisonment of Paul in Rome. No wonder, then, that Luke-Acts attracts the attention of modern historical-critical scholars.

Yet these scholars do not feel altogether comfortable in the historical terrain of Luke-Acts, any more than the author of Luke-Acts might feel comfortable in the mind of modern historical-critical scholars. The two operate out of a different cultural consciousness in each case, and to some extent at cross-purposes. Luke-Acts displays a theological motivation much more so than an historical one. The historical allusions within the text serve the theology, and both are wrapped in rhetoric that serves to promote the Christian cause and persuade believers and unbelievers alike concerning 'the events that have been fulfilled among us' (Luke 1.1), especially the Christ-event. In this light, therefore, it is apropos to speak of the author of Luke-Acts as a 'Christian narrative-theologian', rather than as 'a Christian historian of the early Church'.

The historical, theological and literary mixture in Luke-Acts presents two corollary challenges to the historical-critical interpreter: (1) to treat the historical allusions and references in respect of this triple mixture; (2) to investigate the historical references without prejudice for their contribution to an understanding of the history of Jesus and the post-Easter Church in the context of the Roman world power.

Moreover, the aim of this chapter is to enquire into key events, persons and places that play a part in the narrative drama and theology

of Luke-Acts. To do so, it becomes necessary first to capture the broad
strokes of the literary-theological schema of the two-volume opus.

Literary-theological-historical schema

The hyphenation of the literary-theological-historical is required, it
seems to me, for a proper understanding of the narrative structure of
Luke-Acts. To investigate one at the expense of the other would violate
the admixture of the work. At the same time, each of the three is
identifiable within the schema, and can be discussed as such. Keep in
mind, though, that the author of Luke-Acts, while interested in the
historical, is not an historian in the modern sense of the term.

Two spheres of history

History in Luke-Acts is neither uni-track nor duo-track (for want of a
better metaphor). Rather, the lines of Lukan history are interwoven and
yet identifiable. To change the metaphor, history in Luke-Acts reveals
itself in two coordinate spheres: salvation history and world history. In
Luke-Acts, the one does not violate the other. Salvation history serves
the larger history for good. It behoves rulers of the Roman world
history, therefore, to recognize the place of salvation history within their
sphere of influence. Similarly, the Church of Jesus Christ (present stage
of salvation history) should recognize its divinely ordered mission to
the larger world.

In the narrative of Luke-Acts both spheres are set forth poignantly,
showing the intersection of the one with the other without blurring the
distinction between them.

1. Salvation history

One major aspect of the schema of Luke-Acts is clear: the Christian
Church, of which the writer of Luke-Acts is very much a part, is
connected with the Israel of God traceable through Judaism. As the
author sees it, God planned the movement of salvation through Israel's
sojourn into the missionary march of the Church of Jesus Christ in the
world. When Simeon took the child Jesus in his arms in the Temple,
he declared, 'this child is destined for the falling and the rising of
many in Israel' (Luke 2.34). As the Luke-Acts drama unfolds the
'rising' of Israel is none other than the rising of the Church in the name
of the risen Jesus, who, as 'Son of Man', went to death 'as it had been
determined' (Luke 22.22; cf. Acts 10.42). Further, in Peter's sermon at

Pentecost addressed to 'Israelites' the same divinely determined plan for Jesus and the church is reaffirmed: 'this man [Jesus], handed over to you according to the definite plan and foreknowledge of God, you crucified and killed by the hands of those outside the law. But God raised him up' (Acts 2.23).

Complementary to the divinely ordered plan of salvation is the fulfilment of Israel's Scriptures. In Luke 4, when Jesus launched his ministry in the synagogue at Nazareth, he declared: 'Today this Scripture has been fulfilled in your hearing' (4.21). Similarly, in his resurrected appearance to the bewildered disciples on the road to Emmaus he points out the necessity of Israel's Scriptures being fulfilled in his person and work: 'everything written about me in the law of Moses, the prophets, and the psalms must be fulfilled' (Luke 24.44). 'Today' is important in Luke-Acts. It bespeaks the self-understanding of the writer and his missionary community. They see themselves as the current benefactors of the life and death of Jesus. The Spirit of that Jesus is theirs 'today'. 'Today' the salvation promised earlier to Israel has come to their house, as it came to the house of Zacchaeus in the ministry of Jesus (Luke 19.9).

The fulfilment motif comes to expression by means of echo and allusion, not only by citation of proof texts. The barrenness of Elizabeth (Luke 1.7) is like that of Hannah in 1 Samuel 1. God removed the barrenness of both women and gave to each of them a son who proved himself a worthy prophet-servant of the Most High. In the case of Elizabeth's son, John the Baptizer, he acted out of 'the spirit and power of Elijah' as he made ready 'a people prepared for the Lord' (Luke 1.17). The same continuity with Israel comes across even more strikingly in Jesus. His identity is knitted into the genealogical fabric of Israel as far back as the Israelite story goes – to Adam and to God (Luke 3.23-38). This fulfilment figure, Jesus, took on the role of the servant of the Lord who suffered redemptively, like the servant of Second Isaiah (Isa. 42.1-4; 49.1-6; 50.4-9; 52.13–53.12). Israel's story of suffering in slavery and in exile finds fulfilment in the suffering death of Jesus. In his body God enacted a new Passover and a new Restoration after captivity (Luke 22.15-18), and passed the result on to the Church through the presence and proclamation of the Spirit-empowered Apostles (Acts 3.18-20).

What can be said of salvation history focused in the Israel of God can be said also of the symbols that so governed the lives of the people. These symbols, not surprisingly, have been reconstituted in Jesus and in the Church called by his name.

Luke-Acts makes much of the symbolism of 'the Twelve'. Jacob's 12 sons were foundational for the Hebrew people on their way to nationhood. Jewish people the world over recognized the significance of the twelve Patriarchs of Israel as the founding fathers of the holy nation. Symbolically, the Twelve in Judaism was a composite reference to the singular Israel, God's chosen people. There can be little doubt that the historical Jesus spoke of there being 12 disciples. And the author of Luke-Acts cashes in on that tradition as belonging to the Church of Jesus Christ 'today'. The Lukan Jesus chose the Twelve (Luke 6.13); the Twelve were with him in his ministry (Luke 8.1); Jesus gave power and authority to the Twelve (Luke 9.1); he instructed the Twelve about his journey to Jerusalem to suffer (Luke 18.31); the Twelve will judge the 12 tribes of Israel (Luke 22.30); the one traitor of the Twelve (Judas Iscariot) is replaced by Matthias to keep the number intact (Acts 1.23-6); the Twelve call the whole post-Easter community in Jerusalem together to make an important decision (Acts 6.1-2). As Paul emerges in Acts (ch. 9) as the principal missionary to the Gentiles, the Twelve slip into the background. What the 12 Patriarchs of Israel were to Judaism, so were the 12 Apostles to the larger Church of Jesus Christ in the world: founding leaders in continuity with the 12 Patriarchs of Israel.

Unique to Luke-Acts is the reference to the seventy [-two]. (Some trustworthy manuscripts read 'seventy-two'.) The story of their appointment as 'other' apostles – i.e. a group of seventy [-two] sent by Jesus on a mission beyond that of the Twelve – appears in the early part of the travel narrative of Luke. Jesus appoints them to go 'ahead of him in pairs to every town and place where he himself intended to go' (Luke 10.1; cf. Luke 9.1ff). After they had completed their mission the seventy [-two] 'returned with joy, saying, "Lord, in your name even the demons submit to us!"' (10.17).

While the case for the symbolic significance of the Twelve in the narrative of Luke-Acts stands on rather a firm footing, the same cannot be said for the significance of the seventy [-two]. Is it possible that the Jewish legend about the 72 Jewish scribes who translated the Hebrew Scriptures into Greek in 72 days lies behind this unique appearance of the distinctive seventy [-two] Apostles? (See the *Letter of Aristaes*, 50, 307.) That translation of the Hebrew Scriptures was thereafter called the Septuagint (Seventy). The author of Luke-Acts was thoroughly immersed in the Septuagint, and no doubt knew how important that translation of the Hebrew Scriptures was to the Jewish communities in the Hellenistic world beyond Palestine. Even though the suggestion may be somewhat speculative, it has merit in the context of Luke-Acts: the seventy [-two] in Luke symbolize Jesus' vision of a mission to Gentiles by Greek-speaking Jewish disciples. Stephen and Philip in Acts represent this group (see Acts 6.1–8.40; 11.19-20). Their Scriptures for that mission would not have been the Hebrew Bible of Palestine, but the Greek translation by the 72 scribes – the Septuagint, ready-made for the Greek-speaking world.

The central symbol of first-century Judaism everywhere was the Temple of Jerusalem. That symbol stands forth in Luke-Acts in bold relief. None of the other Gospels besides Luke make such a showing of the Temple. In conjunction with the Temple certain functional figures take their place: prophets and priests, Jesus and the Apostles. Luke-Acts is at pains to connect the origin of Jesus and the Church securely with everything the Temple represents in terms of God's plan for Israel and the world.

The Temple symbol first appears in the opening chapter of Luke, where the father (Zechariah) and mother (Elizabeth) of John the Baptizer are introduced. Zechariah and Elizabeth were both from a priestly line. 'Both of them were righteous before God', but Elizabeth was barren. When Zechariah 'was serving as priest before God and his section was on duty', he offered incense on the altar in the sanctuary while the people prayed outside (1.5-10). During that solemn ceremony in the Temple an angel of the Lord appeared to Zechariah with the announcement: 'Your wife Elizabeth will bear you a son, and you will name him John' (1.13). He would be filled with the Holy Spirit, and his preaching would be 'with the spirit and power of Elijah' (1.15, 17).

Later, when Elizabeth was in her sixth month of pregnancy, the angel Gabriel appeared to a virgin, Mary in Nazareth of Galilee, with a similar announcement: 'you will conceive in your womb and bear a son, and you will name him Jesus. He will be great, and will be called the Son of the Most High, and the Lord God will give to him the throne of his ancestor David' (1.31-2).

Within these narratives about the origins of John and Jesus, salvation-historical connections are made. John's father is a priest in the Temple of Jerusalem; his mother is a descendant of Aaron the priest, brother of Moses. Jesus' mother from Galilee is a relative of Elizabeth. The two women meet and the child, John, 'leaped in her womb' (Luke 1.41). Thus, both John, the prophetic forerunner of Jesus, and Jesus himself are connected with each other and with the central symbol of Judaism, the Temple of Jerusalem. In addition, the geographic and demographic connection is made between Galilee and Jerusalem, between the place of Jesus' ministry and the place of his salvific death and resurrection.

But these tangential connections with the Temple are not sufficient for the Luke-Acts redactor. Jesus of Galilee must enter the Temple bodily, officially and ceremonially. Ultimately, in the vision of Luke-Acts, this Jesus will become the Temple for the world through the efficacy of the Apostles and the Church. Moreover, at his circumcision on the eighth day in keeping with the Law of Moses (Torah) the child was circumcised and named 'Jesus' ('saviour') in obedience to the word of the angel. By the same Torah regulation about purification (Lev. 12.4-8) and presentation of the first born (Num. 3.13), the parents presented the child, Jesus, to the Lord in the Temple of Jerusalem, and offered sacrifice 'according to what is stated in the law of the Lord' (2.24; cf. Num. 6.10). On that occasion, Simeon and Anna, both Temple prophets, praised the Lord for the child. Simeon's canticle of dismissal in the Temple (called the *Nunc Dimittis*), after his experience of the child Jesus, is one of the great salvation hymns of the New Testament.

> Master, now you are dismissing your servant in peace, according to your word; for my eyes have seen your salvation, which you have prepared in the presence of all peoples, a light for revelation to the Gentiles and for glory to your people Israel. (Luke 2.29-32)

Luke also tells us that the parents of Jesus went from Galilee to Jerusalem every year for the festival of Passover. On one of those visits, when Jesus was 12, he remained behind in the Temple after his parents had started out to their home in Galilee. 'After three days they found him in the temple, sitting among the teachers, listening to them and asking them questions.' When the parents questioned him about his behaviour, he said: 'Did you not know that I must be in my Father's house?' (Luke 2.41-50). Again, the author of Luke-Acts makes a vital theological connection between the person and work of Jesus and the historic-symbolic significance of the Temple: the two, Temple and Jesus, are the abode of Father-God.

This episode in the Temple when Jesus was a boy of 12 is the last until he enters again at the end of his journey to Jerusalem, the setting of his death.

> He entered the temple and began to drive out those who were selling things there; and he said, 'It is written, "My house shall be a house of prayer"; but you have made it a den of robbers.' Every day he was teaching in the temple. The chief priests, the scribes, and the leaders of the people kept looking for a way to kill him. (Luke 19.45-7).

What is noticeably absent from Luke's rendering of this narrative scene is the overturning of the tables of the money changers. All the other three Gospels report this event (Matt. 21.12; Mark 11.15; John 2.15). But not so Luke. Perhaps that symbolic act of Jesus is less fitting to Luke's salvation-historical schema. If Jesus' overturning of the tables in the Temple signals the Temple's destruction, then Luke may want to mute that action of Jesus. The Temple function continues, not within the Herodian precincts merely, but in Jesus alive in the Spirit-empowered community after Easter. For the author of Luke-Acts, the Temple symbolism was not overturned or destroyed, but transferred and transformed into the life and mission of the Christ-community in the world. The sacrificial bodies and blood on the altar in the Temple had become the body and blood of the crucified Christ for the Church and the world. During his last Passover meal with his disciples Jesus left them the immortalized Eucharistic words as he broke the bread and drank the wine: 'This is my body, which is given for you. Do this in remembrance of me. ... This cup that is poured out for you is the new covenant in my blood' (Luke 22.19-20).

Remarkably, the Temple is still present in the early narratives of Acts. Remarkably, I say, because the officials of the Temple-system were instrumental in bringing about the death of Jesus. One would think that with the outpouring of the Spirit of Jesus the Temple would promptly move off the narrative stage of Acts. But that is not the case. The Spirit-infused community in Jerusalem 'spent much time together in the temple', as well as breaking bread together in their homes (2.46). Then in Acts 3, Peter and John, two principal disciples of Jesus, make their way 'up to the temple at the hour of prayer, at three o'clock in the afternoon' (3.1). The two were on their way to the afternoon Tamid service of Temple worship, according to Dennis Hamm. They were making connection between their Spirit-experience of Jesus resurrected and the Tamid worship of God in the Temple of Jerusalem. Ironically, in that same hour of Tamid blessing and prayers they find a poor, lame man at the Beautiful Gate of the Temple begging for alms. The healing power of the Temple had not reached the man in need. But Peter reached out his right hand to the lame man and healed him. The restored man then 'entered the temple with them, walking and leaping and praising God' (3.8; cf. Isa. 35.6).

The implication is that the saving powers of the Temple of God have diminished. They have been transferred to the community of the out-poured Spirit of Jesus, represented in Peter's exercise of divine power to heal the lame man. In Jesus' resurrected life, he had become their priest of the daily Tamid service of the Temple: 'lifting up his hands, he blessed them', in the same way as the Temple priest blessed the people in the afternoon Tamid prayers (see Luke 24.50-3).

Continuity with the Temple of Jerusalem carries through the narratives of Acts. In chapter 5 the Apostles teach repeatedly in the Temple. Finally, in chapter 21 Paul observes the rite of purification and sacrifice required by the Temple, and brings Gentile believers with him to the

Temple (Acts 21.25-6). Trouble ensues for Paul. He is accused of profaning the Temple. But the die is cast. Gentiles have become the benefactors of the Temple in the name of Jesus through the preaching of Paul. In his defence, Paul argues: 'I have in no way committed an offence against the law of the Jews, or against the temple, or against the emperor' (Acts 25.8). In short, Paul's Gentile world mission in the name of Jesus Christ and in the power of the Spirit is not in violation of the Temple of Jerusalem, but in continuity with it.

Much more could be adduced about the salvation-historical schema of Luke-Acts. Suffice it to say that the author of Luke-Acts weaves the story of the Church of Jesus Christ and the Spirit into the story of Israel and Israel's God. The divine plan for the salvation of the world finds its fulfilment in Jesus Messiah and in the apostolic community of the outpoured Spirit. Fulfilment does not mean discontinuity from the symbolic life of Israel, but transformative continuity with that life.

The question now is whether the salvation-historical schema in Luke-Acts intersects with world history operating alongside Israel and the Church. Does the author-redactor make connection in the narrative between the two 'histories'? The answer is Yes, in various ways. At certain points the narrator will make the connection, and at other points one of the characters in the story will serve that purpose.

Our task is to identify points of connection within the narrative, and to assess the historical veracity of references to events and persons in the Roman world.

2. World history

What comes across as important to the author of Luke-Acts is the notion that the events of the good news of Jesus Messiah were 'not done in a corner', to use a quote from Paul's defence before Agrippa and Festus (Acts 26.26). From the beginning until 'today', the good Word of God in the name of Jesus has spread openly and unapologetically from Jerusalem and Judaea through Samaria 'to the ends of the earth' (Acts 1.8).

Jesus' birth was marked by events happening not only 'in the days of King Herod of Judea' (Luke 1.5), but also in the larger Roman socio-economic context. 'A decree went out from Emperor Augustus that all the world should be registered. This was the first registration (Lat. *census*) and was taken while Quirinius was governor of Syria. All went to their own towns to be registered' (Luke 2.1-2).

Gaius Octavius ruled as Emperor of the Roman world from 31 BCE to 14 CE. He was declared Augustus ('revered') in 27 BCE. 'All the world' refers to the occupied provinces of the Roman empire. Presumably some provinces of the empire, in this case Palestine, were not registered.

A census of the population in the provinces served for the collection of taxes on the one hand and for the conscription of soldiers into the military on the other. People registered in their local villages or cities. Otherwise they and their property would be hard to find! To the best of scholarly knowledge there is no documented evidence of a regulation requiring residents living in one area to go to another area to register. The narrative-trip made by Joseph and Mary from Nazareth in Galilee to Bethlehem in Judaea seems to be theologically motivated: Davidic messianic tradition underwrites the narrative.

The time of this census is problematic. It happened, according to Luke, 'in the days of King Herod [the Great] of Judea ... while Quirinius was governor of Syria' (Luke 1.5; 2.2). The problem is that these two rulers do not fit the known chronology. Herod the Great died in 4 BCE, whereas Quirinius was not appointed legate of Syria until 6 or 7 CE. The census Quirinius initiated came after King Herod's son, Archelaus of Judaea, was exiled to Vienne in Gaul in 6 CE. That census, along with the Jewish resistance to it, is well documented. Both the census and resistance to it are mentioned again in Acts (5.37; cf. Josephus, *Ant.* 18.1, 6). Efforts to harmonize the chronology are not convincing. For example, the word 'first' (*prote*) could imply a time 'before' Quirinius was governor of Syria, not 'while' he was governor. The sense is strained. If a census happened a decade or more 'before' Quirinius was appointed legate of Syria, why mention Quirinius at all? In point of fact, the author was not as concerned about precise chronology as modern critical historians are. His interest, rather, lay in placing the saving acts of God in Jesus squarely within this larger world of emperors, kings, governors, census-taking and taxation: the world of Roman rule.

The same is true for the launching of John's prophetic ministry. It happened 'in the fifteenth year of the reign of Emperor Tiberius, when Pontius Pilate was governor of Judea, and Herod [Antipas] was ruler of Galilee, and his brother Philip ruler of the region of Ituraea and Trachonitis, and Lysanias ruler of Abilene, during the high priesthood of Annas and Caiaphas' (Luke 3.1-2a). The question is, where did the author of Luke-Acts pinpoint the beginning of the reign of the Emperor Tiberius to arrive at 'the fifteenth year'? Which calendar did he use? Did he count from the death of Augustus or the vote of the Roman senate? If he used the Julian calendar then the date would be August/September 28/29 CE. Beyond this pinpointing of John's ministry, the other references are merely time-brackets: within the time-frame of Pontius Pilate's governorship, Herod Antipas' rule of Galilee, etc.

The dual high-priesthood of Annas and Caiaphas also presents a bit of a problem. First, only one high priest ruled in Jerusalem at any given

time. Second, the high-priesthood of Annas is separated from that of
Caiaphas by a number of years and several other high priests. Annas
was appointed by the Roman governor in 6 CE, and ruled till 15 CE. He
was succeeded by three others whose reigns were short. Then came
Annas' son-in-law Joseph, called Caiaphas, who ruled the Temple
state from 18 to 36 CE. Moreover, Annas and Caiaphas were the two
dominant high priests of the first third of the first century CE. Perhaps
the author of Luke-Acts wishes merely to connect John's life with
both of these prominent Jewish rulers, together with the various Roman
rulers of the time.

Roman rule and practice come through in various contexts of Luke-
Acts, sometimes in the mouths of key characters and minor characters.
When John the Baptist preaches his word of repentance and baptism,
tax collectors and soldiers come and ask what they should do about
their job-situations in response to his message. Here is the scenario, with
John's response in italics:

> Tax collectors came to be baptized, and they asked him, 'Teacher, what should
> we do?' He said to them, '*Collect no more than the amount prescribed for you.*'
> Soldiers also asked him, 'And we, what should we do?' He said to them, '*Do not
> extort money from anyone by threats or false accusation, and be satisfied with
> your wages.*' (Luke 3.12-14)

Both groups are tied in with Roman practice, except that the tax
collectors are Jewish agents for Roman taxation in the province that
once was the Holy Land of Israel. The soldiers are most likely of
Roman extraction. The point is that both are engaged in a practice that
supports the Roman world power. John's instruction to both groups
implies qualified support of the Roman system: tax collectors should
not take commission beyond the prescribed percentage, and soldiers
should not extort money or threaten or accuse anyone falsely, and
should be content with their wages. This attitude in Luke's John is a
far cry from subversive speech against Roman rule and practice.

On the matter of paying taxes to Rome, Luke's Jesus gives a
somewhat different impression. When spies from the chief priests and
scribes asked Jesus about the legality of paying taxes to Rome, his
action and his answer are ambiguous. He says, '"Show me a denarius.
Whose head and whose title does it bear?" They said, "The emperor's."
He said to them, "Then give to the emperor the things that are the
emperor's, and to God the things that are God's"' (Luke 20.24-5). But
the matter is not dropped there in Luke. The issue of paying taxes to
Rome comes up again at the trial before the Roman governor, Pilate.
In that setting, the Jewish assembly of leaders charged: 'We found this
man perverting our nation, forbidding us to pay taxes to the emperor'

(Luke 23.2). But Luke's Roman Pilate is not convinced by the Jewish argument: 'I find no basis for an accusation against this man', Pilate concludes (Luke 23.4).

On the matter of Roman soldiers again, Jesus' healing of the centurion's servant in Luke is strikingly different from the same story in Matthew. Luke presents the Roman occupation of Palestine in a much more positive light. A comparison of the parallel texts in Figure 3.1 highlights the Lukan view of the interface between salvation history coming through Judaism into Jesus (and the Church) and affecting the Roman power and persona for good. The Lukan redaction-elements are in bold.

Luke 7.2-10	Matthew 8.5-13
A centurion there had a slave whom he valued highly, and who was ill and close to death. When he heard about Jesus, **he sent some Jewish elders to him,** asking him to come and heal his slave. When **they** came to Jesus, **they** appealed to him earnestly, saying, **'He is worthy** of having you do this for him, for **he loves our people, and it is he who built our synagogue for us.'** And Jesus went with **them,** but when he was not far from the house, **the centurion sent friends to say** to him, 'Lord, do not trouble yourself, for I am not worthy to have you come under my roof; therefore I did not presume to come to you. But only speak the word, and let my servant be healed. For I also am a man set under authority, with soldiers under me; and I say to one, "Go," and he goes, and to another, "Come," and he comes, and to my slave, "Do this," and the slave does it.' ... When **those who had been sent returned to the house, they found the slave in good health.**	A centurion came to him, appealing to him and saying, 'Lord, my servant [*pais*] is lying at home paralysed, in terrible distress.' And he said to him, 'I will come and cure him.' The centurion answered, 'Lord, I am not worthy to have you come under my roof; but only speak the word, and my servant will be healed. For I also am a man under authority, with soldiers under me; and I say to one, "Go," and he goes, and to another, "Come," and he comes, and to my slave, "Do this," and the slave does it.' When Jesus heard him, he was amazed and said to those who followed him, 'Truly I tell you, in no one in Israel have I found such faith.' ... And to the centurion Jesus said, 'Go; let it be done for you according to your faith.' And the servant was healed in that hour.

Figure 3.1

Notice especially that the Jewish elders in Luke declare the Roman centurion *is* worthy, whereas Matthew lets the centurion's statement stand: he is *not* worthy. Furthermore, this representative of Roman occupation 'loves our people' and 'built our synagogue for us'. There can be no question that the Lukan redactor here merges world history compatibly with salvation history in unmistakable terms.

Still on the subject of the historical reality of Roman occupation of the province of Palestine by virtue of the military, the centurion at the foot of the cross of Jesus plays a striking role. The Luke-Acts agenda of compatibility between the Christian community of the Spirit of Jesus and the Roman myth of peaceful coexistence (*Pax Romana*) has no better spokesperson than the Roman military man as he pronounces his verdict on the crucified Jesus. In this instance Luke follows Mark, as does Matthew. But Luke changes the internal form of the centurion's speech in Mark to suit his agenda. In Mark the centurion says of Jesus crucified: 'Truly this man was God's Son!' (Mark 15.39; literally, 'a son of a god'). In Luke the centurion speaks for Pilate and for Rome while he praises God: 'Certainly this man was innocent' (Luke 23.47).

The same consciousness of the larger sphere of Roman influence appears in the narratives of Acts. As in Luke, some of the historic references are very specific and can be tested against other records. In other cases the allusions are more general. To the specific ones first.

Acts 18.2 notes the expulsion of Jews from Rome by an edict of the Emperor Claudius. The setting for the note is Paul's arrival in the city of Corinth in the Roman province of Achaia. There he meets up with two Jewish believers in Jesus, Aquila and his wife, Priscilla (cf. 1 Cor. 16.19). The two, being Jewish, moved to Corinth from Italy, 'because Claudius had ordered all Jews to leave Rome' (18.2b). Without getting into the tricky issue of Christians being in Corinth *prior to* Paul's mission there, a word about the edict from Emperor Claudius is of interest. Is there evidence beyond Acts of such an edict at that particular time?

The reign of Emperor Claudius (41–54 CE), including his expulsion of Jews from Rome, is well documented in several Roman annals. For example, the event is recorded in a biography of Claudius written by Suetonius: 'He [Claudius] expelled Jews from Rome, who were constantly making disturbances at the instigation of Chrestus.' Acts says 'all Jews' were expelled from the city, but that is doubtful. All those Jewish people who created the controversy, namely, Jewish Christians like Aquila and Priscilla, are likely in view. The controversy and disturbance would have been perceived as intra-Jewish by the Roman Claudius, not as Jewish versus Christian (a separate Christian community was not yet a reality in Rome, or elsewhere for that matter). The issue of the debate was about Chrestus (Latin), or Christos (Greek), presumably referring to the status of Jesus of Nazareth as Messiah of the Jews. In any case, the edict of expulsion, according to the best calculation, happened in the ninth year of Claudius' reign, which would put it at 49 CE. This date corresponds well with what is known of Paul's arrival in Corinth. He arrived after Aquila and Priscilla had arrived, which was some time after 49 CE.

In the same chapter 18 of Acts Paul was summoned to appear before Gallio, the proconsul of the Roman province of Achaia, to answer a charge brought by Jewish leaders that Paul was encouraging people 'to worship God in ways that are contrary to the law'.

Gallio's term as proconsul of Achaia is one of the best documented pieces of historical information in Acts. An inscription, discovered in a temple of Apollo in Delphi, contains a letter from Claudius to his friend Gallio when he was proconsul of Achaia. By comparing the dating in this inscription with that of another found in Cairo, it is possible to date the time of Gallio's proconsul rather precisely, between January and August of 52 CE. Moreover, Paul's case before the tribunal in Corinth would have occurred in the spring or summer of that year, 52 CE (Paul himself makes no mention of the incident in his letters).

Gallio dismissed the case against Paul with a speech of censure to the plaintiff group to sort out their own religious quarrels without bringing them to the tribunal (Acts 18.14-16). This speech from a non-Christian Roman, in favour of Christians, is one of several such speeches in Acts (e.g. 25.5, 14-21; see below). Furthermore, the speech accents the close relationship between non-Christian Jews and Christian Jews. The speech also implies that privileges accorded Jews in the Roman world should apply equally to Christians.

Other significant interactions with Roman authorities occur in the context of Paul's arrest and trial in Jerusalem and Caesarea. It is not possible here to enter into detailed discussion of the lengthy narrative of the situation, extending from Acts 21.17 to 26.32. Suffice it to say that word about Paul's controversial preaching and practice reached law-observant Jewish believers. They heard he was teaching 'all Jews living among the Gentiles to forsake Moses, and ... not to circumcise their children or observe the customs' (21.21). It was also reported that he 'actually brought Greeks into the temple and ... defiled this holy place'. The Acts redactor corrects the report with the note that some Jews had seen Paul in the city with a Gentile named Trophimus 'and they supposed that Paul had brought him into the temple' (21.28-9).

Judging from Paul's own testimony in his letters, however, the Jewish reaction to him in Jerusalem was not without some justification. Paul repeatedly taught that 'a person is justified by faith *apart from works prescribed by the law*' (Rom. 3.28; 4.2-5; also Gal. 2.16; 3.11). By his own account, Paul had already received the 39 lashes on five occasions from the Jewish leaders in the Diaspora synagogues (2 Cor. 11.24). They must have perceived violations of the Jewish Law in Paul to inflict that punishment on him. He was, after all, incorporating believing Gentiles with believing Jews into covenant community on the same footing, without requiring circumcision, Sabbath-keeping or kosher regulations. That was bound to raise the ire of traditional Jewish leaders in any part of the world, most certainly among those in Jerusalem.

What is important for the present purposes is the way the Jewish-Christian missionary, Paul, intersects with the Jewish Temple, Jewish Law and Jewish leaders, and these together with the Roman power brokers in the province, in particular governors *Felix* and *Festus*, and King *Agrippa*. The attacks against Paul invariably move out of the Jewish court and planned ambush scenes into the Roman tribunal, on the heels of Paul's announcement that he is a Roman citizen (Acts 22.25-8). What about the three Roman-oriented characters and actions in the trial drama of Acts? Is there historical warrant backing their place in the narrative?

Paul was transferred from Jerusalem by the Roman commander, Claudius Lyses, to Governor Felix in Caesarea – the Herodian port city and seat of authority in the province of Judaea. An official letter (23.26-39) from commander Lyses went with the military entourage, to be delivered to Felix upon their arrival in Caesarea with Paul. This letter from one official to a superior reflects Roman law, especially where an appeal is made. Furthermore, Paul's trial before both governors, Felix and Festus, is an example of extraordinary penal procedure in a Roman province.

Now to the character of this Roman Felix first, and to the date of Paul's appearance before him in Caesarea.

Felix appears in the work of Tacitus, under the name Antonius Felix, and in Josephus under the name Claudius Felix. The two writers appear to be referring to the same man. Felix also appears on inscriptions. His name comes up also in Suetonius' *Life of Claudius*. Felix gained Roman freedom from slavery by the good grace of Antonia Minor, mother of Emperor Claudius. Claudius then appointed him procurator, or governor, of Judaea, Samaria, Galilee and Perea. The dates for Felix cannot be pegged precisely from the available evidence. The two outside limits are 52 CE on one side and 60 CE on the other. More likely Felix's term ended some time in 56. Moreover, his governorship in Palestine agrees with the context that Acts presents.

Acts' picture of Felix is somewhat mixed. He is 'rather well informed about the Way' – a term Acts uses to designate followers of Jesus of Nazareth (9.2; 18.25, 26; 19.23; 22.4; 24.14). When he hears from Paul, Felix postpones his decision and orders the centurion to keep Paul in custody, but with some liberty to talk to friends. More negatively, Felix is a conniving character in this narrative. He summoned Paul frequently to converse with him, hoping 'that money would be given him by Paul' (24.24-6). Looks like coaxing a bribe! This negative picture corresponds somewhat with the description in Tacitus, who depicts Felix as cruel and lustful. Josephus likewise paints a rather negative picture of him.

The author of Acts has rightly placed Porcius Festus as successor to Felix. Apart from this narrative in Acts, little is known of Festus. Josephus mentions him in *Antiquities* and also in *Wars*. Emperor Nero appointed Festus to the post. His term ran from 56 CE until his death in 62. Unlike Felix, Festus belonged to an important group of Roman senators. Paul's case was still pending when Festus took office (Acts 24.27).

The most notable point about Paul's court appearance before Festus in Acts 25 is his appeal to the Emperor, who would have been the young Nero at the time – not the most worthy imperial ruler! Paul's defence speech before Festus, one of several in Acts, again declares his innocence, along with his appeal to appear in the tribunal of Rome before the Emperor himself. As a Roman citizen Paul had the legal right to make the appeal. And Festus was legally bound to grant it, if the appeal had valid grounds. Paul had been in prison without official sentence. His case was not getting a fair hearing with the Jerusalem elite leaders bringing the charges. His appeal was as much for a change of venue as it was to a higher court. For the redactor of Acts, Paul's defence before Festus marks the occasion for Paul's journey to Rome to bear witness to Jesus Christ there ('the ends of the earth', 1.8). With Paul's appeal to Festus to move his trial to Rome, the proceedings come to a halt. 'You have appealed to the emperor; to the emperor you will go,' said Festus (Acts 25.12).

But that was not quite the end of the scene between Paul and Festus at Caesarea. The third important Roman figure enters the juristic performance: King Agrippa, along with Bernice. But who is this Agrippa? Where is his realm? What makes him Roman? And who is Bernice? Answers to these questions (albeit succinct) will bring this foray into the Roman world history in Acts to a close.

Agrippa II is great-grandson of King Herod the Great, and son of Herod Agrippa I of Acts 12. Agrippa is called 'king' of the Jews in keeping with the Herodian dynasty of Jewish rulers since Herod the Great. Bernice was sister to Agrippa II, as was also Drusilla, wife of Felix (24.24). Bernice lived in the court of her brother. Josephus recounts the gossip about the relationship of Agrippa II with his sister, Bernice. Later she was involved with Titus, the Roman general who besieged Jerusalem in 66–70 CE.

Agrippa II was born in 27 CE, educated in Rome and took over the territory originally ruled by Philip the Tetrarch, namely Ituria and Trachonitis (cf. Luke 3.1). When Nero came to power he added parts of Galilee and Perea to that realm. By these accounts Agrippa II is 'king' of the Jews. But he is also integrally involved with Roman politics and jurisprudence. Hence his presence in the Roman court of Festus, and his interest in this Jewish believer in Jesus of Nazareth in Galilee.

For the author of Luke-Acts, this trial scene echoes the earlier trial of Jesus in Pilate's court, as recorded in Luke. In that trial, Herod Antipas of Galilee questions Jesus. In this trial his relative Herod Agrippa plays the same part in the Roman court of Festus. For Jesus the trial ended in Jerusalem with his execution. Paul's trial will end in Rome. For each in turn the end is paradoxically the beginning. The author of Luke-Acts knows that very well. He is privy to Paul's lost trial in Rome, no doubt, and to his execution in that city. But Paul, like his Lord, Jesus Christ, continues to preach through the Spirit in the lives of his converts and disciples: in the lives of people like the author of Luke-Acts. No wonder Luke-Acts ends, not with the execution of Paul in Rome, but with Paul 'proclaiming the kingdom of God and teaching about the Lord Jesus Christ with all boldness and without hindrance' (28.31).

Synthesis

Throughout the discussion we have encountered various forms of literary discourse: birth narrative, temple narrative, ethical narrative, trial narrative, defence speech, juristic letter, etc. And we discovered a Luke-Acts schema that ties the beginning of the Christian story (birth narratives) into the symbolic history of Israel, especially the symbolism of the Temple of Jerusalem. And the story continues with the symbolism intact, except that the saving significance of the Temple has been transformed into the community of Jesus Christ. The healing of the lame man at the Beautiful Gate of the Temple is a sign that the new Tamid service of blessing now falls to the hands of the Apostles of Jesus.

When Paul appears on trial for defiling the Temple and perverting the Law of the Jews he defends himself against all such charges. He says to the Roman governor Felix, 'I went up to worship in Jerusalem. ... I worship the God of our ancestors, believing everything laid down according to the law or written in the prophets. ... After some years I came to bring alms to my nation and to offer sacrifices' (Acts 24.10-22). At the same time, he was busy carrying the saving significance of both Law and Temple into the Gentile world in the name of Jesus, the Way. For Luke-Acts the course of salvation history from Israel through Jesus and the Church to the world is unstoppable. The cruel death of Jesus did not stop it, nor will the imprisonment of Paul in Caesarea or in Rome stop it.

While all these episodes of saving history are textured into the text of Luke-Acts, world history (viz. the Roman imperial system) intersects with the ongoing march of the saving acts of God in Israel, then Jesus, then the community of the outpoured Spirit of Jesus. Soldiers are instructed to be content with their wages and not treat people shamefully. Tax collectors in the province of Judaea are not to take more commission than is right. The Roman centurion is 'worthy' of having Jesus heal his slave. The trials of Jesus and Paul occur in Roman courts before Roman governors, who declare them innocent.

While the events of God's salvation are not identical with Roman history, they do occur within the system and can be identified with reference to larger events and figures of world history: times and events of Augustus, Quirinius, Tiberius, Herod, Agrippa, Pilate, Felix, Festus. All this interwoven history happened 'according to the definite plan and foreknowledge of God' (Acts 2.23). Nor is there salvation in any other plan, Roman or Jewish, for 'there is salvation in no one else [than Jesus], for there is no other name under heaven given among mortals by which we must be saved' (Acts 4.12). Moreover, while the author of Luke-Acts may aim to accommodate Rome as far as possible in defence of the Christian Way, he still holds onto the exclusive character of the saving work of Jesus Christ, saviour of both Israel and the world.

Further reading

A number of commentaries provide detailed analysis of the historical data in Luke-Acts. Joseph A. Fitzmyer, *The Anchor Bible: The Gospel According to Luke* (*I–IX*, 1981 and *X–XXIV*, 1985); *The Acts of the Apostles* (1998); Beverly Roberts Gaventa, *Abingdon New Testament Commentaries: Acts* (2003); Hans Conzelmann, *Hermeneia: Acts of the Apostles* (1987). The narrative structure and unity of Luke-Acts is well demonstrated in Robert C. Tannehill, *The Narrative Unity of Luke-Acts: A Literary Interpretation* (1986 and 1990); for the 'speech-form' in Acts, see Marion L. Soards, *The Speeches In Acts* (1994); for the Temple service in Luke-Acts, see Dennis Hamm, 'Tamid Service in Luke-Acts' (2003), pp. 214–31.

Review questions

1. Why would it be appropriate for an understanding of Luke-Acts to hyphenate 'literary-theological-historical'?
2. Illustrate the intersection of salvation history and world history.

3. How important is the Temple of Jerusalem in Luke-Acts?
4. What symbols, other than the Temple, bespeak the salvation-historical schema operating in Luke-Acts?
5. Give two examples from Luke and two from Acts in which the Roman world history overshadows the history of salvation through Jesus Christ.

4

Social-science scenarios:
where people think and live

The historical-critical approach to reading biblical texts invariably underwrites the more recent approaches to reading those texts. Even when some interpreters decry the bankruptcy of historical criticism they are at the same time obliged to recognize its place behind their effort to go beyond it. Social-science interpretation, the model most closely aligned with the historical-critical method, moves more deliberately, and in some respects imaginatively, into the everyday thought and behaviour of Mediterranean people groups identified in the texts.

The social sciences have played a significant role in enhancing understanding of contemporary cultural groups. And now an increasing number of biblical scholars are appropriating the social-science disciplines – especially anthropology, sociology and psychology – to illuminate the patterns of Mediterranean life embedded in the biblical texts. This appropriation calls for some caution, however. It is one thing to study a living culture group of people, and quite another to study culture groups existing only in literary and artefactual remains. One is hard pressed to resist the temptation to impose modern cultural characteristics and labels from *living* people groups onto the *narrative* people of two millennia ago. With this note of caution in place, the use of a social-scientific paradigm can lead to valuable insights into otherwise opaque texts.

Social-science interpreters of the Bible use particular terminology to identify patterns of thought and behaviour operating in the lives of Mediterranean people in their places. Once this terminology is securely in mind, and ready for application to texts, social-science interpretation comes quite easily. In the investigation of the selected texts from Luke-Acts below, I will set out in **bold** type the social-science labels that seem to apply. These labels, properly understood, can then be applied to other texts.

Samaritans

One of the striking features of Luke-Acts is the prominent visibility of Samaritans. These people, so named because of their **geography** – the region of Samaria – do not appear at all in the other two Synoptic Gospels, except for a negative note about them in Matthew 10.5: 'enter no town of the Samaritans'. Beyond Luke-Acts, Samaritans figure in only one chapter of John (ch. 4) in the New Testament. In Luke-Acts, however, Samaritans appear in several different contexts, and doubtless play some theological role in the Luke-Acts schema. But that topic goes beyond our assignment in this section of the chapter, which aims to apply social-science scenarios to texts in Luke-Acts in which Samaritans participate along with other groups of people.

Luke 9. 51-5

[Jesus] set his face to go to Jerusalem. And he sent messengers ahead of him. On their way they entered a village of the Samaritans to make ready for him; but they did not receive him, because his face was set toward Jerusalem. When his disciples James and John saw it, they said, 'Lord, do you want us to command fire to come down from heaven and consume them?' But he turned and rebuked them.

In-group/out-group thinking surfaces in this text. Ancient agrarian life was community oriented. The vast majority of the people lived in village communities, not in urban centres. In-group/out-group mentality was a way of life. An in-group could be identified by **geography** – Galilean, Judaean, Samaritan – or by some smaller village marker. Geography, among other things, was a **purity marker**. For Judaeans committed to the Temple of Jerusalem, the region called Samaria was off-limits. A loyal Judaean would walk miles around the territory of Samaria rather than risk polluting his person with Samaritan dirt. In this text of Luke 9 Jesus and his in-group (disciples) go through the region of Samaria *en route* to Jerusalem. Jesus 'set his face to go to Jerusalem'. This is a Hebraic way of saying he had made up his mind to go to Jerusalem, but through Samaria. The Samaritan villagers knew somehow that 'his face was set toward Jerusalem'. And that made him part of the out-group, and therefore not worthy of hospitality in their Samaritan village. In other words, the Samaritans knew that the Jerusalemites had drawn the boundary around themselves to the exclusion of the Samaritans. Samaritans had done likewise.

The reaction of the disciples sprang from a loss of **honour** in the presence of the Samaritans. Their response to such treatment was to call down fire from heaven on the Samaritan villagers, in the manner of the prophet Elijah's action. But Jesus rebuked his in-group. The rebuke could be construed as a sign of Jesus' break with, or at least disavowal of, the **honour/shame** scenario that so permeated ancient Mediterranean life.

Luke 17.11-16

Jesus was going through the region between Samaria and Galilee. As he entered a village, ten lepers approached him. Keeping their distance, they called out, saying, 'Jesus, Master, have mercy on us!' When he saw them, he said to them, 'Go and show yourselves to the priests.' And as they went, they were made clean. Then one of them, when he saw that he was healed, turned back, praising God with a loud voice. He prostrated himself at Jesus' feet and thanked him. And he was a Samaritan.

Several social constructs are textured into this text. It is primarily about **healing and health care** in Palestine. Healing in ancient Mediterranean life was not simply about restoring a person's physical ability to function, to earn a living. Illness was very much a social concern. Illness was seen as **deviance** from the social norm. An illness reduced the person to a low status in the group and could lead to the exclusion of the person from the community, depending on the nature of the illness. Leprosy was such an illness. While it may not have been the leprosy of the present time, it was probably a noticeable skin disease that made the person unclean. Once it was recognized as such, the **purity/pollution** code would swing into play: the unclean person had to be excluded from the community. The Jewish Law specified that lepers had to be put outside the camp of Israel (Num. 5.2-3), and should cry 'unclean, unclean' when someone came near them (Lev. 13.45). If they should be healed of their illness they had to show themselves to the priest to verify the fact and then wash several times over a period of seven days. If the person was proven clean after that, then they could return to the camp (Lev. 13.49).

Jesus was a traditional, social healer, not a professional physician. He had prophetic powers to cast out unclean spirits and restore people to a state of purity, ready for renewed status in the community. The request from the ten lepers has as much to do with restoration of social acceptability as with physical healing of a disease.

But there is also the matter of **geography** in the story. Status is also determined by location. The place 'between Samaria and Galilee' is hard to find on the map. It looks like 'no-one's land', a place for **outcasts** or **expendables**. The ten are neither Samaritans, nor Galileans, nor Judaeans. They belong to the group 'lepers' and cannot therefore claim any geographical location as their social place, as they once did. Nine of the lepers were probably Galilean-Jewish at one time, while one was Samaritan and 'foreigner' to the other geographically located nine.

Only the Samaritan returned to thank Jesus. He did not go to a priest, nor did Jesus insist that he go in the end. After all, he was Samaritan. Why would he show himself to a Jerusalem priest? For that matter why should he go to a Samaritan priest? Jesus had become his true healer-priest, and as such could declare him clean, saved from the **shame** of his illness.

Luke 10.25-9

Just then a lawyer stood up to test Jesus. 'Teacher,' he said, 'what must I do to inherit eternal life?' He said to him, 'What is written in the law? What do you read there?' He answered, 'You shall love the Lord your God with all your heart, and with all your soul, and with all your strength, and with all your mind; and your neighbour as yourself.' And he said to him, 'You have given the right answer; do this, and you will live.' But wanting to justify himself, he asked Jesus, 'And who is my neighbour?' [Jesus answers with the parable of the Good Samaritan, 10.30-7.]

The question of **neighbour** was an important one in ancient Mediterranean society. A neighbour was one who shared the same value system, which could include the same language, religion, customs and geography. The parable in this text addresses the question of neighbour, but the parable is framed by an interesting narrative context (vv. 25-9 and vv. 36-7). The assumption is that the interlocutors are Jewish, one a lawyer and the other a rabbi (teacher). The law in view is the Jewish Torah, not Roman civil law and certainly not the Samaritan Torah. The **language** of both would most likely have been Aramaic, the in-group language of Palestinian Judaism at the time.

The interchange between Jesus and the lawyer is called **challenge–riposte**. If the one to whom the challenge is issued fails to meet the challenge with an appropriate response then the respondent's **honour** is at stake. In this case the challenge comes in the form of a question: 'What must I do to inherit eternal life?' If Jesus should say, 'I don't know', or 'I am not sure', then his status as 'teacher' is dubious. The respondent can reply with another question related to the issue, as Jesus does here: 'What is written in the law? What do you read there?' Then the challenger is challenged. The lawyer responds from the law in which he is expert, and does so correctly. Not satisfied with the draw between them, the lawyer then asks Jesus a further question arising out of his correct answer: 'Who is my neighbour?' This time the reply of

Jesus is not with another question, but with a parable that catches the lawyer in his own challenge. A neighbour for a Jewish lawyer or teacher is above all an Israelite, one committed to the tradition and covenant regulation of ancient Israel. To **love** one's neighbour is to attach oneself to the neighbour and to identify with the neighbour. Love is person-to-person attachment, whereas **hate** is disattachment or indifference. To love a person is to provide oneself with a sense of identity. Unlike our modern self-understanding, which is individualistic, ancient personality and conscience operate within community life and thought. Ancient personality is **dyadic**, oriented towards the other. A person knows oneself by the way others in the community perceive that person.

The parable challenges some Palestinian Jewish mores, which the lawyer doubtless accepted as normative. It challenges the **purity/pollution** code of Judaism, which the priest and Levite epitomize. The accepted purity code of the priest and Levite required that they ignore the victim in the ditch. The appearance of the Samaritan with his extravagant compassion challenges the Temple symbolism represented in the two passers-by. The Samaritan is the **hated** one by Jewish standards, one who is definitely not a neighbour to a Judaean travelling down the road from Jerusalem to Jericho. Who the **bandits** were is hard to say. But there were plenty of them in the land at the time. Peasants who had lost their plot to rich overlords often turned to banditry to sustain their lives and the lives of their families. Presumably the beaten man had something worth taking, something a bereft peasant might consider as belonging to him.

The Samaritan in the story is not poor by any means: he carries oil and wine and money. That makes him a trader, not a likeable person among the peasant population. But he has a heart for victims nonetheless, and spends his resources in binding up the victim. Jewish victims on the road can hardly help but identify with the Samaritan, much against their Jewish grain. And in the end the lawyer has no choice but to ascribe **honour** to the person his group conscience would tell him to **hate**. Who was neighbour to the man in the ditch? Answer: The one who showed mercy. Thus the circle defining 'neighbour' is redefined and the attachment (**love**) unbounded.

Acts 8.5-8, 14-17

Philip went down to the city of Samaria and proclaimed the Messiah to them. The crowds with one accord listened eagerly to what was said by Philip, hearing and seeing the signs that he did, for unclean spirits, crying with loud shrieks, came out of many who were possessed; and many others who were paralysed or lame were cured. So there was great joy in that city. ... Now when the apostles at Jerusalem heard that Samaria had accepted the word of God, they sent Peter and John to them. The two went down and prayed for them that they might receive the Holy Spirit (for as yet the Spirit had not come upon any of them; they had only been baptized in the name of the Lord Jesus). Then Peter and John laid their hands on them, and they received the Holy Spirit.

The geographical designation, Samaria, appears no less than seven times in Acts, most of them in chapter 8. The region of Samaria figures schematically in the commission of the resurrected Jesus to the Apostles (1.8). Yet the one to venture into Samaria in due course was not from among the 'Apostles whom [Jesus] had chosen' (1.2), the ones who received the commission. Philip, instead, was the venturesome one. Philip was one of the seven Hellenistic Jewish believers appointed by the Apostles to serve the needs of the neglected widows (6.5; see the discussion below).

Our concern, first of all, with this text about the gospel of Jesus Christ reaching the lives of Samaritans has to do with **deviance**. Deviance, as we have seen above, can happen through illness. However strange that may seem to modern minds, it was not strange to ancient agrarian minds. Illness was associated with sin, and sin was nothing more nor less than deviance from the path ordained by the god of the group. In Paul's words, sin (deviance) is when people 'fall short of the glory of God' (Rom. 3.23).

But deviance happens in other ways as well, as when some people of the group believe differently, or behave differently. Belief and practice were important for group cohesion. Symbols, rituals and practices served as identity markers. Otherwise group identity runs amok, and that would be serious for any ancient culture group. For example, before Paul's conversion/call, his understanding of his Judaean group identity pushed him to pursue those Jewish Christians who, from his perspective, were deviants from the norm of Palestinian, Judaean belief and practice.

Now back to Philip's work among the Samaritans. His preaching and healing activity led many Samaritans to believe in the person Philip presented to them, Jesus Messiah. Word of this remarkable event in Samaria reached the ears of the Apostles in Jerusalem. News affecting group identity travelled quite fast. Ancient cultures had systems of **networking** that served to keep group identity intact. Word passed from one to the other on their travels.

By all accounts in Acts, the Apostles in Jerusalem acted as the guardians of the new developing community throughout the Mediterranean basin. Any additions to the group from outside quarters had to be cleared through that central authority. (See the next chapter dealing with Acts 15 and the conversion of Gentiles.) Clearly, Philip's word by itself was not authoritative. He was not a primary Apostle. Peter and John were. These two went to Samaria to ensure that Philip and his converts to Christ were not deviant in any way. As it happened, there was a problem: the Samaritan converts had not received the Holy Spirit. For the implied author of Luke-Acts that would be deviance from the norm of Christian community life: the community of the outpoured Spirit.

Interestingly, another Hellenistic Jewish Christian, Apollos of Alexandria, was likewise deviant on the same point in dealing with his converts in Ephesus. They had not received the Holy Spirit either (19.1-7). On this later occasion Paul took on the guardian role that had belonged earlier to Peter and John: Paul corrected the deviance, re-baptized the disciples, laid his hands on them, and they received the Holy Spirit.

Widows

In ancient Mediterranean culture, **widows** were not simply women whose husbands had died. They were that to be sure. But widows entered a different socio-economic status upon the death of their husbands. There was no social security net to keep them from falling into destitution and death, except for the good grace of family and village community, which was not always forthcoming. Widows were vulnerable, often subject to harsh treatment (see Deut. 22.22-3; Ps. 94.6; Isa. 1.23; Luke 20.47). God became their protector (Deut. 10.18; Jer. 49.11; cf. Jas 1.27).

Luke 7.12-15

As he approached the gate of the town, a man who had died was being carried out. He was his mother's only son, and she was a widow; and with her was a large crowd from the town. When the Lord saw her, he had compassion for her and said to her, 'Do not weep.' Then he came forward and touched the bier, and the bearers stood still. And he said, 'Young man, I say to you, rise!' The dead man sat up and began to speak, and Jesus gave him to his mother.

While a woman's attachment to her husband would be strong, her attachment to her son, especially the oldest, was even stronger. She could count on his support for life. To lose a husband to death was bad; to lose a son to death was much worse.

This story about Jesus raising the son of the widow to life is just as much, if not more, a case of restoring the widow to life in the community. Her son was her assurance of a sustainable life. She would not have to beg, and would not be at risk of becoming expendable. 'The Lord saw *her* [and] had compassion for *her*.' He cared about the plight of the widow. Thus, the telling narrative comment comes at the end: 'Jesus gave him to his mother.' The widow could live again.

In this story also we find Jesus violating the **purity/pollution** code in the act of raising the widow's son for her: he touched the coffin of a dead man. Perhaps that is why the bearers stood still. They were probably shocked at the act, just as the lawyer would have been shocked at the social script in the parable of the 'good' Samaritan.

Luke 21.1-4

> He looked up and saw rich people putting their gifts into the treasury; he also saw a poor widow put in two small copper coins. He said, 'Truly I tell you, this poor widow has put in more than all of them; for all of them have contributed out of their abundance, but she out of her poverty has put in all she had to live on.'

Ancient agrarian society by default, it seems, devolved into serious disparity, especially between **rich and poor**. Widows were often among the poorest of society. Their only hope of survival was in keeping their status within the symbol system of their heritage. In Palestinian Jewish society the central symbol was the Temple of Jerusalem. Their God made the divine presence known in that place. Their prayers were heard there. In that place priests accepted the sacrifices for the people and assured them of their standing before God, and of their membership in the community of God's people. The poor widow's contribution to the Temple treasury was her way of maintaining her standing. Jesus saw her put in 'all she had to live on', and passed judgement on the situation. The question is, was he affirming her action as one of great devotion? Or was he decrying the fact that the Temple system exacted 'all she had to live on'? Perhaps the problem the text addresses is the inequity of the social reality of rich and poor. The widow's tiny contribution would be likely to go unnoticed by the elite, while the contribution of the rich would be recognized. Jesus seems to find this social situation of rich and poor, with respect to widows, offensive.

The socio-economic reality in that setting was one of **limited good**. Unlike Euro-American society, where scarcity is rather easily overcome by industry and technology, an ancient agrarian society could not sustain all its members if too many goods went to the few. In a society of limited good, the riches of one meant the poverty of another. Hence the repeated condemnation of those who store up treasure for themselves, like the foolish rich landowner in the parable in Luke 12.16-21. His abundant surplus in his barns meant poverty for some, especially for peasants who lost their land through debt.

The rich–poor problem surfaces frequently in Luke-Acts, and nowhere more provocatively than in the story of the rich ruler who asked about the entrance requirement for eternal life (Luke 18.18-25). Jesus told him: 'sell all that you own and distribute the money to the poor'. But the man went away sad, for he had great wealth. Wealth and the kingdom of God in the vision of Jesus are incompatible. 'It is easier for a camel to go through the eye of a needle than for someone who is rich to enter the kingdom of God.' Ironically, poor widows have a better chance at the kingdom of God than the rich landowners. In Luke-Acts the poor are the blessed recipients of the kingdom of grace (Luke 6.20).

Acts 6.1-4

Now during those days, when the disciples were increasing in number, the Hellenists complained against the Hebrews because their widows were being neglected in the daily distribution of food. And the twelve called together the whole community of the disciples and said, 'It is not right that we should neglect the word of God in order to wait on tables. Therefore, friends, select from among yourselves seven men of good standing, full of the Spirit and of wisdom, whom we may appoint to this task, while we, for our part, will devote ourselves to prayer and to serving the word.'

There are actually four specific groups identified in this text of Acts 6 as belonging to the 'whole community' of 'disciples'. But our interest here is with the situation of one of the groups: the **widows**. The other three groups come up for discussion momentarily.

The widows of one group were neglected in the daily distribution of **food**. Food was a daily affair, especially for the peasant class. Hence, the Lord's Prayer, 'Give us each day our daily bread', is a peasant prayer (Luke 11.3). Why these widows in particular were neglected is not altogether clear. Class, which included language in this case, seems to have played a role. Seldom is there found in Acts a note of dissension in the community of faith in Jesus. The implied author is at pains to mute any sign of division in the ranks. Yet here there is 'complaint' at least. It seems one group was receiving favour over against the other, and the widows of the disfavoured group were caught in the middle, without food. But true to form for Acts, the community rallies in the situation and moves to alleviate the problem. Earlier in chapters 2 and 4 of Acts the rule of a common purse was established. Presumably as the community grew the common purse idea became more difficult to sustain. At any rate, there is some small sign of culture clash within the community of the outpoured Spirit of Jesus here in chapter 6: one group of widows is neglected while another group is supported.

The issue is resolved in the text by appointing a group of **men** from the offended culture group to care for the daily administrative task of looking after the widows' **food**. Men, by virtue of their gender status in that society, had both the experience and the ability to carry out the function. The widow-**women** on their own did not. Now to the other three groups in the text of Acts 6.

Hellenistai, *Hebraioi* and the Twelve

'The early Church', as it is sometimes called, was not one homogeneous group, all members believing and behaving in exactly the same way without conflict. Even the earliest **Jewish** believers in the post-Easter Jesus were not all of one mind, mainly because they were not all from the same cultural context. Evidence of an early clash within the primitive Christ-community in Jerusalem appears in Acts 6 (cf. the next stage of internal conflict in Gal. 2.11-14).

Acts 6.1-6

> Now during those days, when the disciples were increasing in number, the Hellenists complained against the Hebrews because their widows were being neglected in the daily distribution of food. ... 'Therefore, [the twelve said to the community], ... select from among yourselves seven men of good standing, full of the Spirit and of wisdom, whom we may appoint to this task, while we, for our part, will devote ourselves to prayer and to serving the word.' What they said pleased the whole community, and they chose Stephen, a man full of faith and the Holy Spirit, together with Philip, Prochorus, Nicanor, Timon, Parmenas, and Nicolaus, a proselyte of Antioch. They had these men stand before the apostles, who prayed and laid their hands on them.

This text recognizes two distinct groups in the composition of the Jerusalem Christian community. The Greek **labels** given them in Acts 6 are *Hellenistai* and *Hebraioi*. The NRSV simply transliterates the two terms, 'Hellenists' and 'Hebrews' – not very helpful for understanding their function in Acts 6. When Paul in his Letters designates himself as one born of the Hebrews (*Hebraioi*), he probably does not mean by that precisely what Acts means. The issue with the two labels in Acts 6 is one of **language** primarily. Nor should the issue of language be dismissed as an insignificant factor in the life of a community. Language was an important cultural identity marker then, as it is now (witness the bilingual tension between French Canada and English Canada). Jewish people in Palestine probably knew two languages, one related to their religious heritage, Aramaic-(Hebrew), and one related to commerce, Greek. For such Palestinian Jewish religionists Greek was necessary for life in the Roman world, but Aramaic was the language of their **liturgy** and of their Temple **cult**. Moreover, the language of Palestinian Jewish identity was Aramaic, not Greek. Those who spoke Aramaic as their primary language, who worshipped in that language, who read their Scriptures in Hebrew, and offered their sacrifices in that language, quite naturally believed that traditional language to be a watershed marker of first-class Jewish identity.

There can be little doubt that the Twelve fall under this description. They probably knew Greek. Their situation under Roman occupation required as much. But they were almost certainly born into Aramaic-speaking families in Jewish Galilee. Moreover, in addition to their specific distinction as 'the Twelve', or 'the Apostles', this special group belonged to the *Hebraioi*. They knew and practised the language of the liturgy and cult of Jerusalem. That leaves the question, who were the *Hellenistai* among the primitive Jerusalem-Christian community?

Even though their label might lead to the conclusion that they were simply Greeks (*Hellenai*) who adopted the Christian faith and joined the Jerusalem-Christian community, Acts does not support it. According to Acts, as also the Letters of Paul, the Gentiles did not enter the new movement of Christ-followers until years later. These *Hellenistai* were, rather, Greek-speaking **Jewish** residents of Jerusalem who had accepted the message about Jesus crucified and raised. They would have come from some other city of the empire to live in Jerusalem, perhaps to end their days there as loyal Jews in the Holy City. Loyal yes, but not Aramaic-speaking. Coming from some other part of the world to Jerusalem, their one language would have been Greek. Hence their label, *Hellenistai*. Their Scripture likewise would have been the Greek translation, called Septuagint, and their prayers would have been spoken in Greek. They probably had their own meeting place for worship. But, along with the *Hebraioi*, they were believers in Jesus Messiah.

The *Hellenistai* in the text are the ones who complained about their widows being neglected. And they complained 'against the Hebrews (*Hebraioi*)', presumably because the widows of the *Hebraioi* had their needs met while the widows of the *Hellenistai* were neglected. But the complaint may have been thus lodged against the *Hebraioi* because the *Hebraioi* held the balance of power in the community by virtue of their number, or of their status as Aramaic-speaking Jerusalemites.

What is striking in the text is that the group selected to deal with the matter are not from the *Hebraioi*, but from the *Hellenistai*. All seven men have Greek names, having come from a Hellenistic cultural background. The Twelve appoint the seven to the task of serving tables, while the Twelve, for their part, devote themselves 'to prayer and serving the word'.

But it is not long (in the narrative) until two of the appointed seven *Hellenistai* begin to preach the word themselves. Stephen distinguishes himself as an ardent Hellenistic Jewish Christian evangelist. His open (liberal?) stance as a Hellenistic Jewish Christian irritates his more conservative Jewish counterparts. When they brought Stephen before the council in Jerusalem, the witnesses said: 'This man never stops saying things against this holy place and the law; for we have heard him say that this Jesus of Nazareth will destroy this place and will change the customs that Moses handed on to us' (6.13-14). But Stephen's vision and preaching were unstoppable. His speech in chapter 7 challenges the unique sanctity of 'this place', namely the Jerusalem Temple, and thus also the Torah that legislates worship in 'this place'. The response to Stephen's speech was violent. His speech threatened the established cultic order in Jerusalem, and he paid the price with his life, as Jesus had done before him. 'And Saul approved of their killing [Stephen]' (8.1).

Philip is the second from the list of seven to venture out beyond the bounds of Jerusalem into Samaria (see above, under 'Samaritans'). His Hellenistic background, like that of Stephen, seems to have enabled him to move into territory beyond the Palestinian geography. It was Philip who met up with an African treasurer, helped him understand the prophecy of Isaiah, led him to faith in Jesus Christ, and baptized him on the spot beside the wilderness road to Gaza (Acts 8.26-40).

It is fairly safe to say that the persecution recorded in Acts 8 was levelled against the *Hellenistai* of the Jewish Christian community in Jerusalem. Acts is not completely explicit on this point, but the inference one could draw from the clues in the text is that the 'severe persecution' Stephen suffered was then directed against his kind, the *Hellenistai* of Jerusalem. 'All except the apostles were scattered throughout the countryside of Judea and Samaria.' The tell-tale phrase, 'except the apostles', speaks volumes. The Apostles were Palestinian Jewish Christians, probably still devoted to the Temple (see Acts 3), and worshipping in the Aramaic language. They, and other *Hebraioi*, were not as subject to persecution from their Jerusalemite authorities at this stage of the Church's development.

In conclusion, the cultural configuration of the developing Christian movement changed as the *Hellenistai* were pushed north. They ended up, not only in Samaria and Gaza, but also in Antioch of Syria. From that centre, on the fringe of Palestinian Jewish society, the Gentile world mission was launched. From Antioch, not Jerusalem, the transformed Paul received the impetus and blessing in the Spirit to break through to Gentile minds and hearts with the gospel of Jesus Christ. Even Barnabas, of Jerusalem persuasion, and John Mark likewise, could not withstand the zeal with which the Antioch community embraced and extended and gospel of Jesus Christ (Acts 12 and 13). Cultural boundaries, together with the characteristic labelling that goes on invariably in cultural groups, began to dissolve, thus allowing people of difference to enter the new community of Christ on the same footing: repentance and faith in Jesus and receiving his Spirit. Eventually Paul was able to say, 'there is no longer Jew or Greek, there is no longer slave or free, there is no longer male and female; for all of you are one in Christ Jesus' (Gal. 3.28).

Further reading

The joint effort of Bruce J. Malina and Richard L. Rohrbaugh on interpreting the Synoptic Gospels is invaluable: *Social Science Commentary on the Synoptic Gospels* (1992). See especially 'Luke', pp. 279–413. Jerome H. Neyrey (editor) brought together in one volume 13 essays by nine specialists on social-science models for interpreting Luke-Acts. This is a very useful instrument: *The Social World of Luke-Acts: Models for Interpretation* (1991). Martin Hengel's book on the period, *Between Jesus and Paul: Studies in the Earliest History of Christianity* (1983), sheds much light on the early period depicted in the first chapters of Acts. His insights on the *Hellenistai* proved particularly helpful for my analysis of the subject. Beverly Roberts Gaventa's commentary on Acts 6.1-7 deals admirably with the social place of widows, and also with the identity of the *Hellenistai: the Acts of the Apostles* (2003).

Review questions

1. Locate all the terms in **bold** type throughout the chapter and explain their significance as social-science labels applicable to the narrative material in Luke-Acts.
2. What is the relationship between geography and people groups, such as Samaritans?
3. What evidence is there in Luke that the Lukan Jesus challenges the social reality in Palestine related to rich and poor, neighbour and widows?

4.   Explain the tension that language can create in religious settings, using the narrative of Acts 6 as illustration.

5

Socio-rhetorical texture: membership in the new people of God

Social-science interpretation has added significantly to our understanding of people, places, institutions, conventions and behavioural ideas encoded in the biblical texts. But biblical texts consist of particular, intentional language. They are, therefore, literary creations. As such the biblical texts function with purpose in keeping with their texture. This is where socio-rhetorical interpretation comes in. Recognizing the gains made by social-scientific investigators, biblical interpreters can further examine the literary tapestry that gives the text its rhetorical force within its social environment.

Aspects of the socio-rhetorical approach

Vernon K. Robbins has pioneered the socio-rhetorical method, claiming that his approach is more integrative than other more specific literary or social-scientific approaches. At the same time, Robbins admits that the texture of given texts will signal the extent to which the socio-rhetorical approach should be negotiated. According to him, texts could exhibit as many as five identifiable textures as follows:

1. *Inner texture* involves particular vocabulary that will evoke feelings, responses, argument, judgement. Key words will be repeated with progressive nuance. The text-unit (pericope) will have an identifiable opening and closing within which the speech-action and storytelling will unfold to create an effect on the reader-respondent.
2. *Intertexture* bespeaks the presence of texts from outside the text woven into the text. Allusions and echoes of known literary-cultural material can be detected in the 'new' text. Social and cultural intertexture will appear here and there, thus tying the text to its contemporary context. An interpreter should expect to find

historical intertexture as well: i.e. events and persons from outside taking their place within the narrative structure. This literary phenomenon is called intertexture in that the texture of the present text, while deploying data from outside, is a 'new' text. The language will generate response in accordance with its own rhetorical texture.

3.   *Social and cultural texture*, not the same as social and cultural intertexture, consists of the capacity of this particular literary creation to challenge its readers to act or react in some specific social and/or cultural way. The call of such a texture is for a change of social and cultural location, as in the challenge to evaluate the social norms and live by a new value system within a given locale.

4.   *Ideological texture* takes into account the viewpoint, or philo-sophical stance, the text and the interpreter mount in the process of interpretation. A feminist interpreter could be expected to react to an androcentric (male-oriented) texture in a text. In short, ideological texture has to do with positioning. The text will exhibit a position on particular issues, and the interpretation will do likewise, sometimes taking a position in opposition to the value-position woven into the texture of the text.

5.   *Sacred texture* refers to literary elements that bear on the relationship between the human and divine. A text may commu-nicate something about gods, spirit beings (such as angels or demons), salvation history, religious conversion, faith community, and the basis for morality. Biblical texts, because they arise out of a deliberately religious setting, manifest a multi-faceted sacred texture. Recognition of this sacred texture in texts should not be equated with a theological interpretation. Theological interpretation asks essentially, 'How then shall we think and live in community in the world in relation to the text and to its tradition in relation to the divine?'

With these five aspects of the socio-rhetorical approach before us, it is time now to enter into dialogue with texts in Luke-Acts, using this approach as appropriate.

Two texts, Luke 2.21-33 and Acts 15.1-35, bear witness to the important issue of membership in the new people of God in relation to Jesus Christ. What is the entrance requirement? What makes the membership authentic? Will the participants be saved in the end? The new community of Jesus Christ in Luke-Acts, as we have seen already, is rooted in the Israel of God expressed in the Jewish religious tradition centred in Jerusalem. It should come as no surprise, therefore, that the traditional marks of inclusion and identity in the Jewish community should be at issue for the inclusion and identity of potential members of the new community of Jesus Christ. If the connection with Israel is to be maintained, then the traditional marks of inclusion and identity are bound to be a matter of debate and discussion. Four marks of inclusion and identity, according to the Law, were prominent at the time of launching the Gentile world mission: (1) circumcision of males; (2) Sabbath-keeping by all; (3) dietary regulations observed by all; (4) separation from idol-pollution by all. Of these four, circumcision was the physical sign of entry into the covenant Israel of God. The other three were signs of having been admitted into full communion with Israel. Paul set the **first three** aside to allow Gentiles to enter into full communion with the people of Jesus Christ (see Rom. 2.25-9; 4.1-12; 1 Cor. 7.19; Gal. 2.11-14; 4.9-11; 5.6-11). The fourth remained intact: 'Flee from the *worship* of idols', he told his converts at Corinth (1 Cor. 10.14, italics added). The *eating* of idol food was another matter (1 Cor. 8.1-13; see discussion below).

The mark of circumcision became especially vexing for Paul in his effort to incorporate Gentiles into Christian community on an equal footing with Jewish believers. His Gentile male converts were adults. For them the prospect of their circumcision was offensive, if not barbaric. To require circumcision of Gentiles was more a deterrent than an advantage to the success of Paul's mission. Painfully aware of the resistance of adult Gentiles to circumcision, and despite his awareness of the covenant legislation to Abraham (Gen. 17.9-14), Paul set circumcision aside as a requirement for the admission of Gentiles into covenant community of Jesus Christ. This much we know for certain from Paul's letters to the Galatians and the Romans. Luke-Acts reveals awareness of this Pauline tradition about the circumcision of Gentile converts and the tension the issue generated within the Jewish-Christian community at Jerusalem.

With this introduction to the subject of membership in the new people of God in relation to Jesus Christ in place, we may now proceed to a socio-rhetorical interpretation of the two texts that deal precisely with the issue of circumcision.

In the interest of economy of paper, I will not set out the two texts in full. Repeated reference will be made to specific texture. Moreover, it is imperative that the student-reader have the text open before them while they engage in the application of the socio-rhetorical approach. At this point it would be a good idea to stop reading this text in order to read the two texts in Luke-Acts, Luke first, then Acts immediately following (Luke 2.21-33; Acts 15.1-35). When you are finished, we shall explore the socio-rhetorical texture of Luke 2.21-33.

Luke 2.21-33

We begin with an examination of the **inner texture** of Luke 2.21-33. This passage is situated within what is generally called the Lukan infancy narrative of Jesus (1.26–2.52). The text opens with a specific time reference in relation to the birth of Jesus, 'after eight days had passed'. This takes the narrative out of the shepherd-and-manger narrative into a ceremonial religious setting. The time signal was well known in Jewish circles, and serves well as an opening. The narrative closes with the parents of Jesus being amazed at what was said about him in the ceremonial religious setting. Between this opening and closing is a narrative array of characters, places, direct speech, Law, Temple and so on. But what is the subject of the whole?

The subject is related to the 'eight days': 'It was time to circumcise the child'. Any Jewish reader, or an informed Gentile reader for that matter, would know immediately what circumcision signified. Circumcision was not merely for medical or hygienic reasons, but for highly charged religious reasons. Circumcision was the mark of incorporation into the people of Israel according to the covenant that God struck with Abraham. What is noteworthy here is that this same subject of circumcision for incorporation into Israel is precisely the subject of Acts 15, which deals with the incorporation of Gentiles into Israel in the name of this same Jesus.

Repeated words tell a tale of their own. In conjunction with other words in the tapestry they reveal their literary will. Figure 5.1 will help to highlight the place and performance of key words in the texture of this text.

The point of putting the operative words of the texture into diagram form is not to 'reveal the meaning'. On the contrary, such a conscious identification of words in a text has the effect of holding back a quick decision about the meaning of the text. When the principal terms of reference are laid out – and the layout is not absolute – then questions of their place and connection within the texture can be asked authentically.

For example, the word appearing most often in this text is 'law' (four times). Clearly there is only one 'law' in view, the Jewish Law (Torah). In that Law circumcision is prescribed for all Jewish male infants of eight days, born into a covenant family of 'Israel'. The Law is first said to be the 'Law of Moses' (v. 22), but is soon depicted as 'the Law of the Lord' (v. 23). As the narrative progresses, the 'holy' Law becomes associated with the 'Holy Spirit' and with 'Israel'. Above all, though, Jesus is the principal figure in the narrative drama. By his circumcision, Jesus is identified with 'the Law', 'Israel' and finally with 'salvation' (*soterion*, v. 30). The whole setting is one of 'salvation'. Who will be

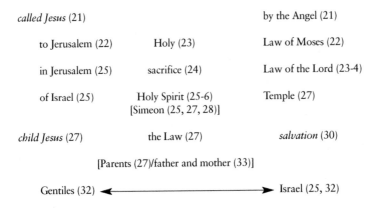

Figure 5.1: Time to circumcise the child

saved? How will they be saved? Significantly, the Hebraic name 'Jesus' (from Hebrew 'Joshua') captures the notion of the salvation of the Lord. And circumcision is the sign of that salvation. All this inner texture begs the question: Who will be saved? And how?

Remarkably, 'Gentiles' appear at the very end of the narrative scene. And as soon as they do they are immediately related to 'Israel'. The two constitute 'all peoples' (v. 31), and 'all peoples' become the potential recipients of God's salvation through this Jesus, circumcised according to the Law at Jerusalem in the presence of the Holy Spirit.

The inner texture of this text does not display any internal opposition. The characters – Jesus, the angel, his parents, Simeon – all belong to the one God, the one Law, the one Holy Spirit, the one Temple in Jerusalem. The amazement in the parents, which closes the passage, arises out of 'what was being said about him' (v. 33). What was being said came from Simeon's speech about Gentiles, Israel and the salvation of both through Jesus. The statement from this Simeon is vouchsafed by his character: 'this man was righteous and devout, looking forward to the consolation of Israel, and the Holy Spirit rested on him' (v. 25).

The one question the inner texture raises *implicitly*, but does not answer, is this: Will the Gentiles have to be circumcised, as Jesus was, in order to be saved? That question will remain in the background of Luke and Acts until Acts 15. Paul's Gentile mission brings it to the fore for resolution.

As for **intertexture**, Luke 2.21-33 incorporates direct speech and allusions from the Jewish Law. 'Every firstborn male shall be designated holy to the Lord' comes from Exodus 13. The act of designating, or redeeming, the firstborn is a memorial to the action of God in saving the people of Israel from the hand of Pharaoh: the firstborn of Israel were saved while the firstborn of Egypt were destroyed. The Luke text updates the memorial, making Jesus' presentation in the Temple the sign of a renewed way of salvation.

The second direct quotation, 'A pair of turtledoves or two young pigeons', comes from Leviticus 15.28-9. This specified sacrifice appears at several points in Leviticus as the offering of those who cannot afford a greater sacrifice, such as a sheep. But the specific text that Luke quotes at verse 24 is Leviticus 15.28-9. That reference speaks specifically about the appearance of worshippers at the tent of meeting for 'purification' on 'the eighth day'. Both terms of reference set the context for the development of the whole text. God is holy, set apart from sin, hence the purification of the worshippers, as they present themselves and their firstborn, from all defilement.

An echo of Leviticus 12.2-3 comes through in the opening line of the text where 'eight days' and 'circumcise' find expression. The Leviticus text reads: 'If a woman conceives and bears a male child, she shall be ceremonially unclean seven days; as at the time of her menstruation, she shall be unclean. On the eighth day the flesh of his foreskin shall be circumcised.'

'The Lord's Messiah' (v. 26) draws on a tradition of the re-establishing of a Davidic dynasty in Israel. At the time of Jesus – and more so at the time of Luke-Acts – the prospect of a new Israel in the land of Palestine was an unfulfilled hope. Still, the people with that history kept the tradition alive, believing that the Anointed (Messiah) of the Lord would appear to reconstitute Israel by the will of God, not by the will of Rome.

There is also in this text **social and cultural texture**. That is, the text calls for a reconsideration of the scope of God's salvation. Israel had kept itself distinct from the other nations. Hebraic culture had been clashing with Hellenistic culture for many years. Israel, as expressed in first-century cultic Judaism, kept itself 'holy' unto the Lord. The separation had deepened with the years of clashing. The social, cultural challenge of this text is to consider the possibility of 'the Gentiles' from a Hellenistic culture and '[God's] people Israel' from a Hebraic culture jointly receiving the salvation of the Lord, and the two together praising the glory of God as Simeon did (cf. Eph. 2.10-15).

The **ideological texture** within the text comes through in the appeal to the Holy Spirit. Throughout Luke-Acts the Holy Spirit is the uniting power and presence in the one new community. The same Holy Spirit existed from the beginning and continues to empower the Church made up of Jewish and Gentile believers in Jesus Christ. The Holy Spirit makes the connection with the past possible, while empowering the community of Christ to move forward in history.

As a postmodern, North American, male, Gentile, Christian interpreter of this text, I am aware of these self-imposed ideological labels at work in the process of my interpretation. I have learned in my cultural context, for example, to reject outright any form of racism. The very notion that one nation, or race, should consider itself superior to another is repugnant to me. And that makes my reading of this text, which nuances the idea of 'Gentiles' and 'Israel', potentially less sympathetic than it should be.

Little needs to be said about the **sacred texture**. It forms the major pattern in the tapestry of Luke 2.21-33. Right away we encounter the 'angel', a heavenly being that communicates the divine will to human minds. Jerusalem and the Temple therein together constitute sacred space. They are 'holy', as Israel is, as the Law of the Lord is, as the Spirit is, and as Jesus is in the end. This text deals with the quest of all human quests: How does a human person in any culture achieve salvation out of the confusion and depravity that so plague the human family? How does one become a member in the people of God on their way to salvation?

Acts 15.1-35

Again, I must emphasize the importance of having the text of Acts 15 open, immediately accessible for cross-checking with the discussion in this section. Chapter 15 is generally entitled 'The Jerusalem Council/Conference'.

The narrative discourse of this passage in Acts is often called the 'turning-point' in the missionary drama of Acts. Certainly the decision-making, dramatized poignantly in the complex narrative, is critical for the success (or failure) of the Gentile world mission. Of course, the issue of God's acceptance of Gentiles has come up already at Acts 10. Through the vision of Cornelius, a centurion and God-fearer on the one hand, and Peter's vision of the sheet of unclean animals on the other, the Gentile and Judaean met under the one roof of a Gentile home. Cornelius received the Holy Spirit and was baptized. That narrative already established *God's choice* to call and create *a people* out of the Gentiles in similar fashion to *the people* first called under the name 'Israel'. But the issue of circumcision in relation to God's acceptance of Cornelius simply did not come up in chapter 10, except to say that 'the circumcised believers who had come with Peter [to Cornelius' house] were astounded that the gift of the Holy Spirit had been poured out even on the Gentiles' (10.45).

Acts 15, however, focuses the matter of the circumcision of Gentile converts specifically, arising as it did out of Paul's attitude and action of incorporating Gentiles without that covenantal mark. Noteworthy here are the points of connection between the narrative of Luke 2 (discussed above) and this narrative in Acts 15.1-35. The exercise of using the socio-rhetorical analysis on the two texts, both of them dealing with the same topic of circumcision in two different situations, could prove fruitful in revealing a pattern of thought in Luke-Acts.

The **inner texture** of Acts 15.1-35 reveals a remarkable overlap of key terms of reference with Luke 2.21-33. The words underlined in Figure 5.2 are those having appeared already in Luke 2.21-33. It can hardly be an accident that no fewer than eleven words appear in the texture of both texts. But Acts 15 also introduces new terms that signal a new situation in the life of the emerging community of Jesus, and with the new terms also a textual feature not found in Luke 2, namely, *opposition* expressed in terms of 'places' and 'persons' and 'beliefs' about membership in the new people of God.

The text is organized into four narrative units. The *first* introduces the subject of the circumcision of Gentiles in order for them to be saved (vv. 1-5). The *second* consists primarily of Peter's speech-argument on the subject (vv. 7-11). The *third* part is a very short narrative *about* the speech of Barnabas and Paul, how their experience among the Gentiles was fruitful (v. 12). The speech itself is withheld. And the *fourth* clinches the matter with the speech of James that culminates in his resolution and decision, usually referred to as the 'apostolic decree' (vv. 13-21).

One of the hallmark features of the inner texture of this narrative is its variety of literary forms embedded within: (1) *direct quotation* from 'certain individuals' from Judaea who remain nameless: 'Unless you are circumcised according to the custom of Moses, you cannot be saved' (v. 1, see also v. 5b); (2) *Peter's oration* about God's decision to include Gentiles with Israel (vv. 7-11); (3) *James' oration* in support of 'Simeon' speech, with the addition of his decision and decree (vv. 13-21); (4) an *ecclesiastical letter* from the Jerusalem church to the Antioch church containing the degree drafted by James.

One of the features of this narrative that distinguishes it from Luke 2.21-33 is the element of *opposition*. In the Luke text there was none at all. The characters were all of one mind; they were all in the same sacred space; the act of the circumcision of Jesus was not at issue. But here in Acts 15, while the subject of circumcision is in focus as it was in Luke 2, the tone within the texture is one of 'no small dissension and debate' (15.2) over the practice of incorporating Gentile believers at

Judaea/Jerusalem (1, 2, 3)	Moses, Law (1, 5)	Antioch (22, 23, 30, 35)
individuals/Pharisees (1) (5)		the brothers (1)
circumcise (1) (5)		Gentiles (3)
		Gentiles (7)
Peter (Simeon) (6, 14)	Holy Spirit (18)	
	Barnabas and Paul (12)	Gentiles (12)
James>Simeon (13)	Holy Spirit [Stated Decree (20)]	Gentiles (14, 17, 19)
Dwelling of David (Israel) (16) [Letter Decree (29)]	All other peoples (17)	Gentiles (17)
SAVED (1)	LORD JESUS CHRIST (11, 26)	SAVED (11)

Figure 5.2: To circumcise the Gentiles or not?

Antioch into community along with Jews without requiring the traditional mark of incorporation, circumcision.

The opposition is depicted in Figure 5.2 by left-side/right-side optics, with Jerusalem heading the left and Antioch heading the right. Under each of the place names are representatives of the stance, with some representatives more to the left and others more to the right. Notice that James is somewhat more to the left than Peter (Simeon), and Barnabas and Paul more to the right than either of the other two. The unnamed 'individuals', and 'believers ... of the Pharisees' (who may be the same persons) are fully to the left, while the 'brothers' and the 'Gentiles' are fully to the right. Between these two opposing sides is the issue of conflict in process of resolution: How are Gentile people incorporated into the Jewish-Jesus community on their way to salvation?

The reference point in the discussion is the Law of Moses, as it was in Luke 2.21-33. That sacred authority calls for the circumcision of all who would join the Israel of God. The 'certain individuals' of Jerusalem stand, therefore, on a rather firm footing in their appeal to circumcise believing Gentiles at Antioch. One wonders what the implied audience might be thinking as they read this narrative. If they happened to have the first volume of this two-volume work in mind (or in hand) they could point, as we can, to Luke 2, which narrates positively the circumcision of their Lord, Jesus. The question is this: Was the circumcision of Jesus a model for all who would be his disciples? Should Paul and Barnabas do for the Gentiles what Jesus' parents did for him? Or did the circumcision of Jesus mean that 'enlightened' Gentile disciples of Jesus would not have to be circumcised? The resolution work-out in the narrative of Acts 15 simply shifts the focus away from circumcision (left-side), and onto the choice of God to include Gentiles (right-side) without 'placing on the neck of [those] disciples a yoke' they would not be 'able to bear' (v. 10).

It is no accident, it seems to me, that James in his speech refers to what '*Simeon* has related' (v. 14). His reference to Simon Peter as 'Simeon' has puzzled scholars. Where Peter is identified by his other name in Luke-Acts, the spelling is 'Simon' consistently. But here it is 'Simeon'. This spelling is the Greek way of saying the Hebrew name 'Simon'. The function of the name 'Simeon' in the texture of this text is that it harks back to the earlier text in Luke 2 where another Simeon blesses Jesus and declares that in Jesus the Gentiles will see the light and enjoy salvation in covenant with Israel. Even though the character with the name Simeon in Acts 15 is a different one from the one who blessed the child Jesus, the implied audience of Luke-Acts would be likely to remember the declaration of the earlier Simeon.

The important part of the inner texture of Acts 15 is the repeated decree – found also in another context at Acts 21.25. Its first appearance comes in the speech of James thus:

a. to abstain only from things polluted by idols
b. and from sexual immorality
c. and from whatever has been strangled
d. and from blood. (v. 20)

The whole church in Jerusalem seems to have endorsed the decree drafted by James (v. 22). They chose 'Barsabbas and Silas, leaders among the brothers' to deliver the decree to the community at Antioch in the form of a letter, an accepted practice in Graeco-Roman society. The letter restates the decree, with some revision: the sequence of the stipulations is rearranged, and the operative word about idols is changed thus:

a. that you abstain from *what has been sacrificed to idols*
d. and from blood
c. and from what is strangled
b. and from sexual immorality. (v. 29)

The change in the sequence is of little consequence, although it does seem strange not to keep sexual immorality (*porneia*) immediately next to the statement about idols. The two, idolatry and sexual immorality, were interrelated in Jewish religious thought. More substantive is the change of wording in the first line from 'things polluted by idols' (*tōn alisgematōn tōn eidolōn*) to 'what has been sacrificed to idols' (*eidōlothutōn*). In the *statement* of James the emphasis is on defilement that comes from any association with idols, which could mean also association with people who worship idols. But the text of the *letter* to Antioch uses a more specific word pointing to food that has been offered to an idol. Such food would end up in a market (*agora*) for sale. Presumably the text of the letter stipulates that believing Gentiles not eat food associated with the worship of idols. This stipulation presents a bit of a problem when we consult Paul in his letters. More on that point later.

The middle two stipulations in the text of the letter come out of a Jewish understanding of how animals should be slaughtered so as to avoid ingesting blood. Strangling tended to hinder the blood from draining completely. The stipulation arises directly out of the Torah regulation against eating blood (Lev. 7.26ff).

The **intertexture** that figures into the narrative weave of Acts 15 is striking and plentiful. Principally – and usually with such subjects – the language of Scripture aids in setting forth the case. Peter's speech, in appealing to God's decision to include Gentiles in relationship with Israel, echoes texts that depict Israel's rebellion against God and their inability to take on the yoke of the Law (Exod. 15.22-7; Num. 14.22; Deut. 6.16; Isa. 7.12; Wis. 1.2). The Law as 'yoke' is positive here, as elsewhere in Luke-Acts (Luke 2.22-4; Acts 21.17-26). The image of the 'yoke' is from the ancient agricultural practice of hitching two animals together for work in the fields (Sir. 51.26; *Mishnah Berakhot* 2.2, 5). Closer to home in Acts, although not characteristic of Luke-Acts, verse 11 seems to carry an echo of Paul's preaching about being saved by grace through faith (see Gal. 2.16; 3.2; Rom. 3.28). The NRSV translation is less than clear. Literally, the text reads: 'through the grace of the Lord Jesus we believe to be saved, in the same way as those also'. That is, 'we' Judaeans and 'those' Gentiles.

But the intertexture in the speech of James is more explicit and to the point at hand. He cites the LXX version of Amos 9.11-12, it seems, although echoes of Jeremiah 12.15 and Isaiah 45.21 come through as well. The focus in James' citation of the Amos text is on rebuilding the house of David by including the Gentiles in the programme. The rebuilding, for Luke-Acts, means Israel reconstituted by having both Judaean and Gentile people come together in one community under God in the name of Jesus. But the question remains: What is the mark of inclusion and identity in this reconstituted Israel? The answer to this specific question, with which the narrative opened, is still not forthcoming. In the end, the decree of James satisfies the Jerusalem demand without requiring circumcision.

One might also think of **intra-texture** in Acts 15. As noted earlier, the vocabulary and subject matter of Luke 2.21-33 figures into the literary world of Acts 15. An intelligent reader of the two volumes could hardly miss the interrelationship between the two texts. Furthermore, the interface between Jerusalem and Antioch in Acts 15 is reminiscent of a similar interface between Jerusalem and Galilee in the Lukan ministry of Jesus (Luke 10–18), and between Jerusalem and Samaria at the time of Philip's mission there (Acts 8). The motif of the 'narrative journey' between Antioch and Jerusalem appears to be carried forward from the journey of Jesus from Galilee to Jerusalem in Luke involving a resolution of tension between those two places and their Jewish peoples. The journey in Acts 15 resolves the tension between the Jerusalem Jewish believers in Jesus and the Antioch Gentile believing 'brothers'.

The most obvious **social and cultural texture** of Acts 15 is that which seeks to transform a long-standing conflict between what Gregory Dix calls Syriac and Hellenic cultures. Clearly, Gentiles will not be included if they continue to practise polytheism, the worship of many gods represented in created things (idols). They will not be included if they engage in sexual immorality, probably referring to sexual practices associated with some Gentile shrines. In short, the Gentile believers at Antioch will have to give up what had been their religious-cultural practice for generations, and take on some of the Jewish regulations regarding eating food. The Jerusalem believers, by contrast, give up nothing of their belief and practice, and take on nothing of the Gentile culture. They will still circumcise their children and observe the Law of Moses. Nothing in Acts 15 indicates otherwise. The issue pertains only to the means by which *Gentiles* are incorporated into the community of Jesus Christ. It is possible *to infer* that for Luke-Acts the circumcision of Jesus, his presentation in the Temple of Jerusalem, and the acclamation from Simeon (Luke 2.21-33) renders the circumcision of Gentiles who believe in Jesus unnecessary.

The text of Acts 15 exhibits a Jerusalem Jewish **ideological texture**. If Gentiles are to be included in the salvation of God, they must conform to the decision of the Jerusalem community. Even though God chose to include Gentiles, the decision of the Jerusalem church by the mouth of James becomes the standard by which Gentiles will be saved. The Law of Moses remains the law for Gentiles, interpreted by the Jerusalem leaders as 'good to the Holy Spirit and to us' (15.28). What might seem good to the Holy Spirit and the Antioch 'brothers' must pass the test at Jerusalem. In this sense, then, the ideology that guides the narrative of Acts 15 is that the Jerusalem-Jewish centre wields authority for all. From there the Christian missionary activity in the world is set on course.

One might compare this ideology, and the decree that grows out of it, with the Christian world-view represented in Paul's letters. Paul's letters show theological respect for the place of Jerusalem in the divine plan of salvation for the world. But Paul does not regard the custodians of the Jerusalem Christian tradition to have any greater authority than he has (Gal. 1.6–2.14), especially when it comes to the incorporation of Gentile believers into the community of Christ. Furthermore, if Paul knew of the decree of James – and according to Acts 15 he would have known – he ignored the decree in his mission among the Gentiles. In 1 Corinthians 8 and 10, where the subject of eating food offered to idols comes up, Paul shows no knowledge of any decree. He instructs his converts at Corinth to 'eat whatever is sold in the meat market without raising any question on the ground of conscience, for "the earth and its fullness are the Lord's"' (1 Cor. 10.25). In some respect, Acts mounts a case for the rehabilitation of Paul within the Jerusalem-Jewish religious context. Paul followed his call to gather the Gentiles into community in the name of Christ in the power of the Spirit. But his liberating action in doing so put him in serious tension with the Jerusalem-Jewish believers, and more so with the non-believing Jewish leaders in Jerusalem.

Sacred texture is plentiful again in Acts 15. The Law of Moses is distinct from the Law of Rome. God gave the Law to Moses as gift to the people called by God's name. Jerusalem continues to be sacred space, whereas Antioch of Syria is not. The Law and Jerusalem are counterbalanced by the Holy Spirit. There is no contradiction between the Law and the Holy Spirit in Luke-Acts. The Sabbath of verse 21 is sacred time, a time of worship in the synagogue. Of course, 'our Lord Jesus Christ' (v. 26) is singularly sacred in the narrative dealing with issues of the believing community.

Conclusion

From this socio-rhetorical analysis of Luke 2.21-33 and Acts 15.1-35 we sense the tension associated with the emergence of the new community of Jesus out of its original home in the environs and context of Jerusalem Judaism into a polytheistic Gentile environment. Luke-Acts ensures the connection between the implied Gentile readers and historic Israel. But the composition of the developing community poses a challenge to that salvation-historical connection. The issue is one of inclusion and identity. What makes the new community, composed of Gentiles along with Jews, the people of God in fellowship with the historic people of God, Israel? What marks do the Gentiles take on in addition to faith in Jesus to render them 'Israel' along with their Jewish counterparts?

Finally, the issue is one of maintaining relationship between uncircumcised Gentile believers and circumcised Jewish believers. More than that, the newly composed community faced the challenge of maintaining identification with the Jewish community that chose not to believe in Jesus as Lord and Saviour. These issues hover in the background of the two texts reviewed in this chapter. From the perspective of this present time, we have to acknowledge the parting of the ways between Judaism and Christianity by the end of the second century, and the subsequent failure of the Christian Church to relate charitably to the Jewish people.

Further reading

The socio-rhetorical approach is discussed fully in Vernon K. Robbins's two volumes, *Exploring the Texture of Texts* (1996), and *The Tapestry of Early Christian Discourse* (1996). On the status of James see Richard Bauckham, 'James and the Jerusalem Church', in *The Book of Acts in its Palestinian Setting* (1995), pp. 415–80. Useful insights come from Fitzmyer, 'The circumcision and manifestation of Jesus', in *The Gospel According to Luke* (1981), pp. 418–33, and Gaventa, 'A conference in Jerusalem', in *The Acts of the Apostles* (2003), pp. 210–27. For a wider scope on the subject see Robert Maddox, 'Jews, Gentiles and Christians', in *The Purpose of Luke-Acts* (1982), pp. 31–65; and Jacob Jervell in *Luke and the People of God* (1972).

Review questions

1. What is implied in the label 'socio-rhetorical'?
2. What are the five aspects of the socio-rhetorical approach to reading biblical texts?
3. What are the socio-rhetorical links between Acts 15 and Luke 2.21-33?
4. Describe the intra-textual role the name 'Simeon' plays in the two passages.
5. How do you understand the opposition present in the texture of Acts 15? And the absence of it in Luke 2.21-33?
6. In what way is the decree of the Jerusalem church different from the practice of Paul reflected in his missionary letter to Corinth?

6

Narrative discourse: poor and rich
in Christian community

To read Luke-Acts as narrative discourse is not quite the same as reading it through the lens of socio-rhetorical criticism employed in the last chapter. A narrative reading does indeed take persuasive elements (rhetoric) of a text into account, but a narrative analysis probes more specifically those features of a literary work that make it 'narrative', as compared to argument, hymn, prophetic oracle, etc. Socio-rhetorical reading can apply equally well to all these literary types, as it can to a Gospel story of the trial of Jesus. A narrative reading, however, applies particularly to a text that displays literary characteristics of an account, whether historical or fictional, that involves such elements as time, place, movement, characters, plot, cause and consequence.

This depiction of Luke-Acts as narrative discourse raises several questions that call for explanation and demonstration: What constitutes narrative? Is it in keeping with the content and character of Luke-Acts to call this composition a 'narrative'? How appropriate is it to apply modern narrative criticism to an ancient biblical composition?

The second part of this chapter will *demonstrate* narrative discourse analysis, with specific reference to Luke 14.1–16.14 and Acts 4.32–5.11. These two texts highlight a prominent concern running through both volumes: the relationship between poor and rich in a community of friends of Jesus Messiah. But before getting there, narrative discourse needs to be *explained*. Throughout the discussion in both parts, answers to the pertinent questions noted above should become apparent.

What is narrative discourse?

A narrative requires a **narrator**. In the case of Luke-Acts, several narrators can be identified. A narrator should not be confused with the 'real author', or historical author (discussed in Chapter 2). The narrator is a creation of the historical author, and may indeed carry out some of the interests and purposes of the historical author. But the narrator speaks within the literary work, along with other speakers, aiding the reader in understanding what is going on. This 'whispering wizard', as she/he is sometimes called, keeps the imaginative movement on track, fills in the reader on some details while leaving some gaps, and generally draws up the terms of reference for reading this particular literary creation. The narrator can be an all-knowing third-person participant, or a more intimate first-person-singular informer ('I'), or a communal first-person-plural comrade ('we'). In Luke-Acts we find all three types of narrator (e.g. Luke 1.1-4; 6.6-11; Acts 1.1-5; 2.5ff; 21.1ff; 28.1ff).

A narrative requires **characters** and **characterization** thereof. It is the narrator's job to identify the characters that play a part in the imaginative movement from one point of departure to another. The characters may have specific names, such as John, Mary, Peter, or they may have label names, such as Samaritan, Priest, Pharisee, Sadducee. A literary character can be a group. Disciples are a group character, as are Pharisees, tax-collectors, sinners, servants, the rich and the poor. Characters are not merely anonymous figures like those appearing on a video monitor automatically in a retail store. For characters to be players in the narrative dynamic, they have to be characterized. And that is the function of the narrator. A character may be described as tall, wearing a coat, walking with a limp. Or a character can be depicted by attitude and action: loves money, is suspicious, greedy and so forth. Again, the narrator provides enough characterization to make the characters serve the purpose of the narrative.

A narrative requires **plot** structure. An earmarked beginning, middle and ending tie the inner workings together. But plot involves conflict resolution, among other matters. The movement will take into account something of a past, while projecting a future. The narrative present then works towards a way forward, using interaction between the characters to advance the imaginative movement.

Beyond these 'required' ingredients for a composition to be called 'narrative', there are several other considerations.

One can speak of an **implied author** within a narrative. That is, the interests and purposes narrated can be translated – but cautiously – into concerns the writer had for his **implied readers**. This pursuit of implied author and implied readers comes from a reading of the narrative, not from some external exploration of a world outside the text. Nor are the implied readers identical to 'first readers'. There could be a connection, but not necessarily. Implied readers are those the narrative calls upon to imagine the significance of the narrative situation.

Mention of readers leads to another important feature of narrative analysis: **reader response**. What part does the reader play in the production (or performance) of meaning? Readers have to be imaginative to read narrative. For someone to say, 'I just read what is there', is to miss the point and purpose of narrative discourse. Narrative discourse prompts the reader to create an image of reality dictated by the parameters and nuances of the narrative. The reader, in this sense, is co-creator of the narrative. The reader performs in imagination what the narrative urges and initiates through the text.

Involved in the response of the reader to the narrative is the operation of filling in **gaps** in the narrative configuration. Gaps occur where there is ambiguity. For example, in Luke 6.1-5, while Jesus and his disciples were walking through grain fields on a Sabbath day, they plucked heads of grain, rubbed them in their hands, and ate the grain. Some of the Pharisees asked: 'Why are you doing what is not lawful on the Sabbath?' Their question raises another in some readers' minds: What is not lawful about walking through grain fields, rubbing grain in the hands, and eating it on a Sabbath day? One might guess at the answer, and come up with several alternatives. But whatever the guess, the narrative form of the text will allow only so much guesswork. For example, the reader is not free to guess that there was no conflict between Jesus and the Pharisees on the narrative playing field.

Finally, narrative discourse contains **implicit commentary**. We have seen this feature already in the use of the name Simeon – rather than Simon or Peter – in Acts 15. Simeon ironically recalls the earlier prophetic Simeon at the occasion of the circumcision of Jesus. Irony is poignant speech, concealing and revealing at the same time, depending on the insight of the reader. In Acts 3 when Peter tells the lame beggar at the Beautiful gate of the Temple that he has no silver or gold to give him, the reader wonders about the power of Peter to do good to the man. Will Peter's gift exceed silver or gold? On another symbolic-ironic level, the lame beggar is lying at the Beautiful gate of the glorious Temple. Implicitly, the powerful Temple is powerless to give the beggar life; powerless to remove his shame in begging. The moneyless Peter, on the other hand, has the power to lift the man to health and honour.

The last question from above remains: Is it appropriate to apply modern narrative criticism to the ancient literature of Luke-Acts? It is appropriate only insofar as Luke-Acts is truly a narrative composition. This composition, more than any other in the New Testament, sets itself up for narrative analysis using the tools of narrative criticism. In the classic prologue to Luke the implied author lays out the parameters of the work, calling it 'an orderly account' (*diēgēsis*, v. 1). In other words, a narrative. He promises in the voice of the first-person-singular narrator to ground this narrative in eyewitnesses and ministers of the word, among other sources at his disposal. Whatever the resources, the end-product will be a narrative, a *diēgēsis*. As such it is subject to a narrative reading, using the same tools of narrative criticism as one would use on a modern novel. This does not deny the existence of historical data embedded within the narrative. But it does acknowledge the authenticity and coherence of the particular *diēgēsis* that is Luke-Acts.

Two documents – one narrative

Before embarking on a close examination of the two narratives (Luke 14.1–16.14 and Acts 4.32–5.11), both of them illustrating the theme of poor and rich in Christian community, it should be noted that Luke-Acts is not a collection of narratives loosely strung together. Nor is Luke a finished narrative. A question remains: Did the disciples stay in Jerusalem after Jesus ascended? Acts answers that question.

The prologues to both books make clear that the two are interrelated, while narrating two distinct phases in the development of the Christian community. The dedication to Theophilus in the Prologue to Luke is repeated by way of allusion in the Prologue to Acts: 'In the first book, Theophilus, I wrote about all that Jesus did …'. But besides this allusion to the 'first book' in the second Prologue, the two are connected by other narrative features, including major narrative themes, such as the rich in relation to the poor.

Luke opens with an infancy narrative set in the poorest of surroundings: a manger in an animal shelter; shepherd visitors; the poorest of offerings at the time of purification and circumcision, all of this under the superintendence of the Holy Spirit (Luke 1–3). Then, after passing a test in the wilderness (4.1-13), Jesus delivers his inaugural sermon in Nazareth in which he reads from Isaiah: 'The Spirit of the Lord is upon me, because he has anointed me to bring good news to the poor. He has sent me to proclaim release to the captives and recovery of sight to the blind, to let the oppressed go free, to proclaim the year of the Lord's favour' (Luke 4.18). He declares the Scripture fulfilled 'today' in their hearing.

From that point forward the Lukan Jesus makes friends with the poor, the lame and the blind; healing and blessing them; eating with them; and telling stories against those who would accumulate wealth. Luke ends with the resurrected Jesus walking along the road to Emmaus with two disciples. He enters their house, making friends with them as they break bread together. They in turn meet up with the eleven apostles in Jerusalem and together they witness the reality and blessing of the resurrected Jesus before he ascends into heaven (24.13-53).

Acts connects with the Lukan narrative, first in the prologue, but also in a revised version of the commission and ascension. From that point onward in Acts the Holy Spirit is the empowering agent through whom all the positive characters carry forward the witness from Jerusalem, Judaea, Samaria and on to the uttermost parts of the earth. The themes of friendship and Christian community continue to occupy the multi-faceted narrative, which ends much as Luke ended: with Paul alive in Rome and bearing witness to the resurrected Lord Jesus.

The ending of Acts is a narrative ending. That is, the principal character, Paul, who brought the gospel to the Gentiles, is alive and preaching the good news of Jesus resurrected in Rome, just as the early Apostles had preached the same news to the residents of Jerusalem in Luke. The implied author of the ending of Acts knows of the two years Paul spent under house arrest in Rome, and knows that the two years have come to an end. How else could he write about the time element? But Paul's physical demise would not serve the narrative purpose of the two-volume work: that the good news of salvation to Israel in the birth of Jesus has reached Rome alive and well through the agency of the Holy Spirit in the missionary persona of Paul.

Costly friendship: losing and finding; scattering and gathering (Luke 14.1–16.14)

The same directive applies here as in the last chapter: read Luke 14.1–16.14 carefully before proceeding to the discussion below.

A word about the layering of narratives in Luke should help set the course. The narrative as a whole is tied together primarily by a third-person omniscient narrator. This is the speaker-director of the unfolding movement in the story from its beginning to its end. This larger narrative schema may be called the *primary narrative*. But the narrator of this large movement surrenders the narrative momentarily to other narrators who tell their smaller stories within the framework of the larger narrative. These may be called *embedded narratives*. In our text (Luke 14.1–16.14), both are present. Jesus tells narrative parables, each one with its own fictional characters. These embedded narratives, told by Jesus, advance the movement of the primary narrative towards its outcome (*denouement*).

Jesus is also the principal *character* in the primary narrative. He is the protagonist, cast alongside others, both opponents and friends. He knows the right path and follows it. He instructs others about the Way to God through sayings, and in dialogue with the various other characters.

Speaking of the Way, it is noteworthy that this text of Luke 14.1–16.14 falls within the narrative journey of Jesus and his friends, the disciples, on their way from Galilee to Jerusalem. As a setting for the distinctively Lukan narrative (9.51–19.27), the journey to Jerusalem is an ironic one: it is a journey of Jesus to death, which leads to newness of life beyond all death. This Way, unlike the mighty Roman roadways, leads, not merely to the capital of the empire, but to the kingdom of God. It is within this ironic travel setting that we encounter the plot and characters, and the discourse that makes the narrative Lukan.

Pharisees as foil (14.1-35)

The other characters with Jesus play significant roles in developing the theme and plot related to friendship. Pharisees are a group character, with one Pharisee in particular inviting Jesus to his house for a meal on the Sabbath (14.1, 12). This house meal setting colours the whole discussion about making friends, who they should be and how to relate to them. The Pharisee who hosts the dinner, along with his like-minded guests, is characterized in the narrative as scrupulously law-observant, watching Jesus closely, not able to reply to Jesus' question about healing people on the Sabbath. Jesus then heals the man with dropsy (14.1b-6). The Pharisees seek honour at the expense of the less honourable. They are proud. They invite their own kind to their house, and are suspicious of Jesus as to whether he is one of them or not (14.7-11). They grumble (15.2). And they are 'lovers of money' (16.14).

Characterized thus, the Pharisees act as a foil for Jesus, who counsels his host (a Pharisee) to invite 'the poor, the crippled, the lame and the blind' to the banquet (14.13-14). These words drip with irony. A *banquet* for *these* people? All of them together constitute a group character in Luke. They have no audible voice within the narrative, ironically so, because they have no voice in the society either. Yet there they are, prominently on display in the voice of Jesus, as also in the voice of the omniscient narrator. This fourfold character, representing everything that elite society despises, is the very character that God in Jesus loves.

One of the dinner guests (presumably another Pharisee), 'on hearing this', picks up on the word 'blessed' in Jesus' admonition, and remarks: 'Blessed is anyone who will eat bread in the kingdom of God' (14.15). This guest character may have heard with his ears what Jesus said, but he has failed to understand in his heart. It is his *misunderstanding* that then prompts Jesus to tell the narrative dinner parable in which 'the poor, the crippled, the lame and the blind' figure prominently (14.16-24).

Like all such parables of Jesus, this one activates thought, challenging the accepted wisdom of the day. Big dinners are put on by those who can afford to do so, the rich. The invited guests, like the host, are people of means. One had bought land. Another bought five yoke of oxen. And another has to attend his marriage feast. Ironically, all these invited 'friends' of like means decline the invitation to the dinner. They can do without it. They are not hungry. They have other things to do. But their self-exclusion opens the door for the opposite group to enter the banquet. People in this group are hungry, probably begging in streets and lanes of the city, and in the roads and lanes of the country. These unlikely candidates for a banquet become friends of the rich banquet-provider; they eat at his table, and he becomes their friend *to the exclusion* of the initially invited friends (14.21-4).

The parable, following as it does Jesus' admonition to the Pharisee to invite 'the poor' to the banquet, begs the question in response: Is it possible for the wealthy and the poor to be friends together in one setting? To eat at the same table? To live in the same household of faith in Jesus?

The implied author is posing these questions by incorporating Jesus' narrative parable, and is asking his implied readers about their own form of Christian friendship in their community. If there are rich people in the implied audience they will be pushed by the force of this narrative texture to ponder the implications of having two socially opposite classes in the one community operating under the name 'Christian' (Acts 11.26). Can the two coexist, using this one character label, and be authentic all the while?

The implied author, through the narrator, plots the direction of the desired answer to that question by bringing Jesus back into the primary narrative, which follows the parable (14.25-35). The audience changes as the group travels forward. *Large crowds* become the potential respondents to the question (14.1). Jesus addresses them. Large crowds implicitly consist of different classes of people. Jesus sets up the condition of friendship with him – namely discipleship – in unequivocal terms in his speech that follows. Friendly followers will have to give up family members, even life itself, and carry a cross. For us there is a significant gap in our understanding of 'the cross'. It has become a religious symbol in Christianity, and as such is adored. It was not so for readers in the Roman empire. The symbol of 'the cross' for the implied readers was a symbol of shame ending in cruel death.

The cost of befriending Jesus is high here, as elsewhere in Luke. Anyone who does not count the cost before starting on the journey with him will be put to shame in the end, like the builder of a tower who fails to count the cost, or like the king who goes to battle without counting his soldiers. But what about the rich? What will it cost them to join the friends of Jesus? It will cost them everything they own: 'None of you can become my disciple if you do not give up all your possessions' (14.33).

The gap the reader has to fill in here concerns possessions. One who possesses things, and that legitimately by the accepted standard, who *owns* earthly resources rather than treating them as gift, is denied friendship with Jesus. A possessor of resources, in the company of the dispossessed, cannot at the same time, on the same road, in the same community, be friends together with Jesus. One owns while the other is disowned: disowned by the greed of the rich, like the rich fool in the parable, who gathered surplus for himself without regard for the poor (Luke 12.16-21).

Somewhat puzzling at the close of this pericope (14.25-35) is the image of the good salt that can go bad (vv. 34f). Yet the puzzle is not as opaque as it first appears. This 'salt' is not table salt, sodium chloride, but field salt, perhaps potassium or nitrogen. Such land salt is good as long as it is distributed over the land or the manure pile. Only then is its life-giving worth manifest. Land salt that sits in a pile eventually cakes and loses its potency, 'fit neither for the soil nor for the manure pile'. That is how it is with wealth as well. It loses its potency, much like the undistributed salt. But, lose the wealth by distributing it, and behold, it brings life to an otherwise impoverished people. In turn, the benefactors become friends with the formerly wealthy, friends with Jesus, and friends with God. 'You cannot serve God and wealth' (16.13).

The salt metaphor at the end of Jesus' counsel on what it takes to be among his friends also serves as transition to the next several parables embedded in this primary narrative. The stockpile of salt is *lost*, if it is scattered on the land or the manure pile. But, ironically the salt yields newness of life by that loss. So it is with life in relation to Jesus: 'Those who try to make their life secure will lose it, but those who lose their life will keep it' (Luke 17.33; cf. 9.24). Thus, the metaphor of the salt lost by scattering on the land paves the way for the parables that follow, where loss and scattering lead to gain, where sorrowing and seeking lead to rejoicing.

Tax collectors and sinners as friends (15.1-32)

Another group character enters the narrative scene, tax collectors and sinners. Their appearance heightens the tension between Jesus and the Pharisees, and with good reason. Given the narrative hints at the beginning of chapter 15, this group represents everything the Pharisees despise. And implied readers are obliged to fill in the gap in understanding who these people are. Why are they so despised? In short, tax collectors and sinners epitomized law-breaking. Tax collectors were Jewish pawns of Rome, earning their living by taking commission from the taxes paid to the Roman oppressor. Sinners were those who broke the law by prostituting themselves sexually. They were offensive to the law-observant Pharisees. But these tax collectors and sinners listened to Jesus. In turn, he welcomed them and ate with them. Eating with someone means you are their friend, at one with them. Hence the criticism from the Pharisees: 'This fellow welcomes sinners and eats with them' (15.2).

In response to the criticism, Jesus tells a series of narrative parables about loss and scattering, about finding and rejoicing. It may be appropriate to read these parables not as told solely against the Pharisees, but as also told towards the listening heart of the tax collectors and sinners. The narrator sets up both groups as the audience at the head of the set of parables. That being so, while the Pharisees might feel judged by the parables, the tax collectors and sinners might feel blessed by them. Readers will have to respond out of their own situation in life in relation to the narratives, both the embedded parables and the primary narrative.

What, then, of the parables? The first two are straightforward enough (15.3-10). If someone loses one wandering sheep out of a hundred, he will go after the lost one until he finds it. Similarly, when a woman loses one silver coin out of ten she will search for the lost coin until she finds it. But the ending to both parables is key to the Lukan narrative thread. With the safe return of the lost sheep and lost coin, the finders call 'friends and neighbours' together, saying, 'Rejoice with me'! (vv. 6, 9). Ironically, the loss and scattering of sheep and coin become in the end the catalyst for rejoicing in community, and in heaven.

'Scattering' in Luke-Acts is thematic. It is particularly focused in the case of the 'scattering' resulting from the persecution associated with Stephen's death (Acts 8.1-4; 11.19). Out of the painful scattering comes new community and new life in Christ resurrected. Hints of the same ironic scattering–regrouping appear in all the parables embedded in this narrative, running from 15.1 to16.14.

The next parable, usually called 'the parable of the prodigal son' (15.11-32), is probably the best known and most loved of all the parables of Jesus. (It is also the longest of the parables.) This one certainly qualifies for the 'scattering' motif. The family is scattered in the parable. The younger son scatters (*diakortizō* = squandered, NRSV) his inheritance. But out of the painful scattering comes return, renewed relationship against all odds, and rejoicing with friends and neighbours in a party celebration. Ironically, the older brother did not scatter, nor was he himself scattered. Consequently, he has no sympathy for his wastrel brother and no interest in the feast with friends and neighbours. He has, by his own indifference to the relocated family member, excluded himself from the celebration with friends.

This parable has received super-abundant attention by scholars and church people alike, and is ever open to further insights from different angles. Richard Rohrbaugh's social-science treatment, for example, provides a worthy complement to the many other interpretations (see 'Further reading' below). For the purposes of this chapter, however, the concern is with the narrative function of this embedded, fictional narrative within the primary narrative of Luke-Acts. Like the previous two parables, this extended narrative parable carries forward the same thread of welcoming back lost ones – as a result of scattering – into a circle of friendship where there is feasting and rejoicing in community.

The difference in this longer parable, however, comes at the end where the elder brother becomes angry at the welcome-home party in honour of the 'scattered-lost' brother. Questions that implied readers might ask in response would be: Who would be likely to exclude themselves from a community in which the lost ones are welcomed back with open arms? Is it possible to have the once-scattered rebels and the constantly loyal stalwarts congregate magnanimously around a fellowship meal? Can the two be real friends of each other and of Jesus? Similarly, is it possible for the wealthy and the poor to be friends of each other and of Jesus? This last question leads immediately to our last parable in the series.

Disciples as leaders in training (16.1-14)

When you read the whole series of parables at one sitting it is not immediately obvious how the last one fits with the earlier ones. Yet there it is, grouped with the others by a slim narrative comment, 'Then Jesus said to the disciples ...' (16.1). By means of the sequence connector 'then', the ensuing parable belongs with the preceding ones. But how? This parable seems so different on the surface, its plot structure and action tortuously hard to figure out. Perhaps the narrative character type, 'the disciples', is supposed to be able to tease it out in their learning role in the company of Jesus.

Inside the embedded narrative, usually referred to as 'the parable of the unjust steward' (16.1b-8a), three fictional characters cross the stage: a rich man, a retainer/manager of the rich man's business affairs, and debtors to the rich man. Word reached the rich man that his manager was 'scattering' (*diakortizō* = squandered, NRSV) his property. The word used to describe the charge against the manager is exactly the same word used to describe the action of the prodigal son in disposing of his inheritance. Right away we have a verbal connection between the two embedded narratives. Both narratives present a problem, which ironically becomes the basis for a blessing. The problem in the 'unjust steward' parable, from the perspective of everyday business sense, is in the scattering of property. But there is here also more than a faint flashback to the words of Jesus addressed to the crowds about cross-bearing: 'none of you can become my disciple if you do not *give up* all your possessions' (14.33). How does one 'give up' possessions? Presumably by distributing them, scattering them, forsaking them. The action may look foolish by the conventional wisdom of the world, but it yields the good fruit of the kingdom of God. The manager in the parable has been letting go of the rich man's possessions. Like the majority of Jesus' narrative parables, this one leaves puzzling gaps for the reader. We do not know if the manager was spending the money on himself, or if he was letting the debtors have money that belonged to the rich man. Judging by the manager's behaviour upon learning of his impending dismissal, he had been scattering the money among the debtors. He knew he had lost his job anyway (16.3), so he might as well carry on doing what he had been doing, and thus make friends with the debtors: '[these] people may welcome me into their homes' (v. 4). Again, the note of friendship is implied. And implied readers meeting in house-churches of the first century may bend a listening ear at this point.

The most troublesome part of this parable for modern interpreters comes at verse 8a, when the embedded narrator gives the response of the rich man to the action of the manager: 'his master commended the dishonest manager because he had acted shrewdly'. Internal contradictions stare the reader in the face: How can dishonesty be commended? What is shrewd about doing more scattering of the rich man's money? Is the manager not risking imprisonment by such action? He has exposed himself blatantly. But he has also exposed the rich man at the same time. The rich man seems to go through a kind of conversion. He begins to see the situation in a new light. What was once dishonest becomes the shrewd thing to do: relieve the debtors of some debt, and make friends of people who could otherwise be enemies. What once warranted the manager's dismissal from his position has become *commendable*. A new world opens up to the rich man by observing the scattering policy of the manager. Perhaps something of this reading fits the narrative context of Luke here.

Narrative disciples are listening and learning, as implied members of house-churches should be. The group of parables, and especially the last one, sets the stage for an outflow of moral lessons tailored for disciples, spoken in no less authoritative voice than Jesus'. Layered one upon the other, the wisdom sayings serve as memorable guides for Christian behaviour in the company of friends related to Jesus.

- 'The children of this age are more shrewd in dealing with their own generation than are the children of light' (v. 8b). **Implied response:** scattering managers, converted rich people and relieved debtors can be friends in the same home.
- 'Make friends for *yourselves* by means of dishonest wealth so that when it is gone, *they* may welcome *you* into the eternal homes' (v. 9). **Implied response:** When Jesus-people (*you/yourselves*) befriend dishonestly wealthy people (*they*), the wealthy will scatter their wealth and welcome you, friends of Jesus, into 'eternal homes' (lit. 'tents', possibly an echo of the 'tent of meeting' in the wilderness). To call a tent 'eternal' is peculiar. Perhaps it points to the kind of large home wealthy people can afford, which they may 'give up' to serve as a meeting place for the new people of God in Jesus Christ, and thus gain for themselves eternal life (Luke 18.18-30).
- 'Whoever is faithful in a very little is faithful also in much; and whoever is dishonest in a very little is dishonest also in much. If then you have not been faithful with the dishonest wealth, who will entrust to you the true riches? And if you have not been faithful with what belongs to another, who will give you what is your own?' (16.10ff). **Implied response:** Puzzlement. Which dishonesty is in view here? The commended dishonesty of the manager in the second part of the parable, or the dishonesty of the rich man in the first part of the parable, *before* he commended his manager for scattering his property? This one reading response presents itself: it is good to be faithful in being 'dishonest' by the standard of conventional wisdom (i.e. managers relieving debtors), because that kind of dishonesty (*adikos*) is honesty (*dikos*) by the standard of the kingdom of God. Recall, the manager was commended for alleviating debts owed to his master, which the 'unconverted' rich man had seen as 'dishonest'.

• 'No slave can serve two masters. … You cannot serve God and wealth' (v. 13). **Implied response:** The wealth of the wealthy must serve God by being distributed. That way everyone can be friends in the same house-church.

Pharisees as outsiders (16.14)

From disciples back to Pharisees, the narrative focus shifts to opposition. Pharisees heard all this and ridiculed Jesus for such teaching. The ridicule came not because they perceived a broken rule of Jewish law, but simply because they 'were lovers of money' (v. 14). As such, they are not prepared to distribute their money and thus make friends with new economic equals. By ridiculing the egalitarian Way of Jesus they exclude themselves from the friendship of Jesus expressed in Christian community. So the implied readers would likely construe. Of course, the Pharisees become a narrative cipher for any rich class label in the churches of the Mediterranean basin.

It is time now to examine the selected text in Acts, in which the subjects of property, friendship, community and God intersect.

Costly community: fearful honesty in the disposal of property (Acts 4.32–5.11)

As we read this passage in Acts, after reading the above narrative in Luke, an 'Aha!' feeling comes over us. Now we see the outworking of the *giving up* of property for the sake of true friendship and real community. A hint appeared already earlier in Acts that the principle of a Christian community had begun to take hold (2.44-5). But as with every good and perfect gift in this world, counterfeit lies close at hand.

The voice of the primary narrator carries the movement and description forward, with Peter acting as interrogator of the two negative characters, and as intermediate communicator of their death.

Ideal community (4.32-5)

The omniscient narrator knows the 'the whole group of those who believed' (v. 32). And it was no small group, judging by the thousands that were being added as a result of the apostolic preaching (2.42; 4.4). Line upon narrative line gives testimony to the character of the new community of the resurrected Jesus:

'[they] were of one heart and soul' (v. 32a)
'no one claimed private ownership of any possessions' (v. 32b)
'everything they owned was held in common' (v. 32c)
'great grace was upon them all' (v. 33b)
'there was not a needy person among them' (v. 34a)
'as many as owned lands or houses sold them' (v. 34b)
'they laid [the proceeds] at the Apostles' feet' (v. 35a)
'[the proceeds] was distributed to each as any had need' (v. 35b).

For the narrator of Luke-Acts, this composite picture of the new community constitutes the radical outworking of the vision, words and acts of the crucified Jesus, raised by the power of God. The theme is clearly *oneness*: oneness of heart that creates oneness among the people gathered in the name of Jesus. But this is no pie-in-the-sky spiritual oneness that accommodates anything and anybody in a house of friendship. The oneness of *heart* translates in this narrative into oneness among the human members gathered together for fellowship and worship (cf. 2.42-6). One community in the name of Jesus Christ cannot, by that name, accommodate itself to the needy and the wealthy and still be one. How could both groups offer the same prayer to the ascended Lord? By implication, the prayers – so important in Luke-Acts – would not be the same: one group would be thanking God for property owned, while the other would be begging God for the next meal. In this ideal narrative community of Acts, however, 'there was not a needy person among them' (v. 34), because 'everything they owned was held in common' (v. 32c).

The trustees were the Apostles, who appear also to be the administrators of the common fund. Quite a task! And one that the narrator of Acts later admits was beyond the power of the Apostles to administer equitably: the widows of the Hellenists 'were being neglected in the daily distribution of food' (6.1). Like every ideal, this one was subject to default over time, and even corruption. But Acts (backed by Jesus in Luke) holds up the ideal as a mirror image for readers for all time.

One of the striking features of this narrative is the interplay of different characters. Barnabas acts as positive counterbalance to the negative attitude and behaviour of Ananias and his wife Sapphira. Peter comes through as authority figure, acting on behalf of the authoritative group, the Apostles. Corresponding to the positive–negative interplay on the human level are two characters from the spiritual realm: the Holy Spirit (positive) and Satan (negative). These last two remain backstage, appearing only in the voice of the omniscient narrator.

Barnabas as positive example to emulate (4.36-7)

The description of the oneness of the primitive community in Jerusalem in 4.32-5 functions as context for the introduction of one Joseph, whom the Apostles called 'Barnabas'. His introduction in this highly positive context is apt, because this Barnabas plays a significant role in the development of the community after the massive 'scattering' noted in 8.1ff. He teams up with Paul (9.27), and like Paul is an 'Apostle' (14.14): a missionary extension of the Twelve Apostles, but not quite their equal. Acts regards Barnabas' mediating performance between Jerusalem and Antioch as highly important in safeguarding the continuity between Israel centred in Jerusalem and the extension into the Gentile world. He is present with Paul during the controversy about the incorporation of Gentiles into the new community in Antioch (Acts 15).

But what of his introduction, his characterization, at the end of chapter 4? It is brief but poignant. He is said to be a Levite and native of Cyprus (v. 36a). These two features make him a first-class candidate for the mediating role mentioned above. His Levitical genealogy gives him ready access to the Jewish leaders of Jerusalem, especially the priestly hierarchy. And his home country of Cyprus makes him a member of the Diaspora community. Strangely, though, according to Jewish Law Levites were not supposed to own land in Israel (Num. 18.21-4; Deut. 18.1-4). Barnabas did own 'a field'. The field may have been in Cyprus, and therefore not subject to the Law for Levites, which pertained to the land of Promise and to service in the tent of meeting. Furthermore, by the time of the first century that part of the Law for Levites, like the law of the Jubilee year, may have slipped into dysfunction.

This Aramaic name, Barnabas, the Apostles gave serves the narrative function, but only when it is translated into Greek as 'son of encouragement' (*huios paraklēsis*, 4.36). Without the narrative translation the Aramaic name means 'son of (*bar*) the prophet (*nabas*)'. There is no telling what the Aramaic etymology might have meant initially. Nor does the implied author provide the slightest hint. His narrative interest is in portraying the character of this Joseph Barnabas as a positive model for anyone who would join the community of Jesus Messiah. Barnabas sold his field and brought the money 'and laid it at the Apostles' feet' (4.37b). This phrase, 'Apostles' feet' – repeated three times in this passage (4.35, 37; 5.2) – carries an implicit comment: the Apostles are authority figures to whom the other members of the community submit. In this case members submit their money, but implicitly they submit themselves to the Apostles' leadership.

Ananias and Sapphira as negative example to shun (5.1-11)

Apart from their appearance in this highly charged narrative, this couple is otherwise unknown in Acts or elsewhere in the New Testament. Their appearance here, however, confirms one rather unhappy reality: that even the Christian community can become tainted by counterfeit and deception. When that happens, says the narrator in so many words, judgement on the perpetrators is swift and severe.

The two characters enter the narrative stage separately, seemingly to establish the idea that their action was contrived. They contrived together to keep back part of the proceeds for themselves. But was their sin in keeping part of the proceeds? Or was it in the contriving to lie about it? Perhaps a bit of both, but mostly the latter.

Ananias brought the money and laid it at the Apostles' feet, in the same submissive manner as Barnabas. But unlike Barnabas, Ananias concealed his contrived thought and action from the apostolic community, and thereupon came under scrutiny of the apostolic insight and word of Peter.

Peter is pictured here as gifted with a kind of sixth sense. He calls Ananias to account for lying to the Holy Spirit, prompted thus *in his heart* by Satan (v. 3). These two otherworldly characters epitomize the positive–negative polarity. Satan, as spirit, can fill the human heart of a believer in Jesus, much as Satan filled the heart of Judas who betrayed Jesus for money. On the other hand, the Holy Spirit of truth, also capable of filling the human heart of a believer, does not tolerate the lie. Here is the indictment of Ananias: 'you did not lie to us but to God' (v. 4b). And the punishment for his sin: instant death! (v. 5).

The story is somewhat reminiscent of the one about Achan in Joshua 7. This man too kept property for himself from the fallen city of Jericho, which was supposed to be consecrated to the Lord. His sentence was likewise death, but not by the hand of God directly, as seems to be so for Ananias, but at the hands of 'all Israel' who stoned him to death and burned his property. If there is *intertexture* here between Joshua 7 and Acts 5.1-6, it seems more an echo than deliberate interplay.

As noted above, the entrance of Sapphira after her husband confirms the deceit and establishes her complicity in the act of lying to the Holy Spirit of God. Peter's enquiry of her was – one might say today – a trick question. If he knew immediately that Ananias had lied about the amount of the proceeds from the property, then surely he knew Sapphira carried the lie in her heart as well. His enquiry confirms what he already knows: 'Tell me whether you and your husband sold the land for such and such a price.' Answer, 'Yes, that was the price' (5.8). Peter frames his response somewhat differently this time. He accuses Sapphira of putting the 'Spirit of the Lord to the test' (v. 9). The test was whether the Spirit of the Lord would find out that they had kept part of the money for themselves while giving the impression that they had laid it all at the feet of the Apostles. The punishment is the same for the lying and the testing: instant death! (v. 10).

No wonder 'great fear seized the whole Church and all who heard these things' (5.11). This is the first time 'church' (*ekklēsia*) is mentioned in Luke-Acts. (An *ekklēsia* is literally 'a called-out group'. The LXX uses the term for the congregation of Israel, e.g. Judg. 22.5; Ezra 10.1). The implied church audience could hardly escape the affective power of this narrative. It would be a serious sin to lie to the Holy Spirit by lying to the Church and its leaders. Better to do what Barnabas did: hand over the proceeds honestly without reserve. And above all, the Church of Jesus Christ should be one in heart and soul, which translates into oneness of physical resources. Whatever the personal cost in *giving up* property to be part of the Christian community, membership in that community of the Holy Spirit of God in the name of Jesus Christ is its own reward.

Further reading

The following titles should prove helpful. William S. Kurz, SJ, *Reading Luke-Acts: Dynamics of Biblical Narrative* (1993); William H. Shepherd, Jr, *The Narrative Function of the Holy Spirit as a Character in Luke-Acts* (1994); Robert C. Tannehill, *The Narrative Unity of Luke-Acts: A Literary Interpretation*, vol. I: *The Gospel According to Luke* (1986), pp. 103–39, and vol. II: *The Acts of the Apostles* (1990), pp. 59–79; Ju Hur, *A Dynamic Reading of the Holy Spirit in Luke-Acts* (2001); Richard L. Rohrbaugh, 'A dysfunctional family and its neighbours', in Shillington, *Jesus and His Parables* (1997), pp. 141–64; Paul Trudinger, 'Exposing the depth of oppression', in Shillington, *Jesus and His Parables* (1997), pp. 121–37; William R. Herzog II, *Parables as Subversive Speech* (1994), pp. 233–58; Philip Francis Esler, *Community and Gospel in Luke-Acts* (1987), pp. 24–45, 164–200. Ryan Schellenberg's 'The Parable of the Lukan Steward in Lukan Context' (MA thesis 2005; projected publication 2007) merits mention here, even though it is not published at this date.

Review questions

1.   Describe 'narrative discourse' with reference to the material in Luke.

2. In what ways are the two volumes, Luke and Acts, a unified narrative?

3. How do the embedded narrative parables of Jesus in Luke 14–16 illustrate the 'scattering' (viz. distribution) that brings forth friendship and rejoicing?

4. In what ways is the 'ideal community' of believers in Jerusalem an expression of the vision of Jesus in Luke? How is the 'ideal' corrupted?

5. From your reading of the selected narratives in Luke-Acts, can the wealthy and the poor together be friends of Jesus in the same community of faith?

6. What would be the implied response in a Lukan audience to the character of Barnabas on the one hand, and the character of Ananias and Sapphira on the other?

7

Postcolonial engagement: missionary attitude and activity

A postcolonial reading of Scripture texts is happening, not only among scholars from previously colonized lands, but also among European and North American biblical and theological scholars. Postcolonial interpretation allies itself with other tested approaches, such as the historical-critical method. What, then, is a postcolonial reading of texts?

As the name implies, 'postcolonial' signifies a period after the overt colonial attitudes and practices prevalent from the eighteenth to twentieth centuries. The imperialist practice of invading so-called virgin lands and their peoples was carried out under the guise of civilizing the indigenous people and making the land agriculturally viable. Undergirding this practice was an ideology of superiority, both in terms of race and of power. The power of the colonizers came by virtue of Empire. By its very nature, Empire expands into territory vulnerable to the takeover of the more powerful invaders. But the conquest was not merely political and military. It was also commercial and religious. The East India Company and the Dutch East India Company were examples of commercial colonialism. And with the political and commercial interests and activities came also the Western missionaries with the Western Christian message and Western Christian culture. The whole colonial mix was seen by the conquerors as good and right for the conquered peoples. But the result was one of domination by an alien culture group over an indigenous culture group. Western values and patterns of behaviour were imposed on the indigenous populations of Asia, Africa and South America. Despite the 'post' in 'postcolonial' the attitude and ideology of domination has not disappeared from those enmeshed in Euro-American systems of power. Power-posturing has simply taken on new forms. It behoves all of us engaged in educational endeavours to raise awareness of prevailing remnants of colonialism and imperialism in our socio-cultural structures and practices.

Self-appropriation

Who is in a position to carry out a postcolonial interpretation of biblical texts? Certainly those readers who have survived colonial rule, who have risen above foreign domination and the imposition of Western culture. But even they will have to engage in self-appropriation, to lay their accrued biases on the table with the rest of us, and so read the texts.

Before I approach the missional texts in Luke-Acts, I feel compelled to lay out my own complicity in colonialism, and thus my own struggle to read the texts afresh with the help of others less complicit than myself. Currently I live in Canada, specifically in the city of Winnipeg. This city has one of the largest populations of indigenous people in the country. I see first-hand every day what British imperialism has done to the conquered people of this land of Canada. They are called 'first nations' people: first because they were here before the British or the French. But the 'first nations' are still governed by the dominant Anglo-European majority.

Before coming to Canada in 1958, I was born and reared in Northern Ireland. My Protestant forebears moved from England to the northern province of Ulster in Ireland in the seventeenth century to boost the Protestant population there, and force the native Celtic Catholics into minority subservience. It was called the English Plantation policy. I recall thinking in my teen years in Northern Ireland that I could get a job in the world-famous shipbuilding industry in Belfast, because I was Protestant. My Catholic neighbour could not get that job in that industry, simply because he belonged to the Catholic minority in the British-occupied province of Ulster.

On top of that, I am now, and have been for over thirty years, a member of a privileged group in the West, a tenured professor in a Canadian university. There is no denying that my professorial position in such an institution carries with it a degree of power. Thus, I wonder if I am in a position to interpret texts that have for generations been subjected to a colonialist reading, a reading that promoted missionaries of the eighteenth, nineteenth and twentieth centuries in their evangelistic journeys to foreign lands on commercial ships funded by the imperialist merchants. I would like to think I have undergone a conversion that enables me to take up an appropriate postcolonial posture while engaging the texts of Luke-Acts. It remains to be seen whether or not the conversion really happened.

There are two sides to a postcolonialist interpretation, as I understand it. One is the attitude and ideology of the interpreter and the other is the attitude and ideology embedded in the text. Both these sides will come into play in the process of the ensuing postcolonial reflection. Luke-Acts, as we have seen already, was written during the heyday of Roman colonization and occupation, and exhibits leanings toward Roman jurisprudence and social order. Moreover, a postcolonial reading of Luke-Acts involves reading against the grain. The aim overall is the transformation of heart and mind (my own and the reader's) towards freedom to think through and act out the good and the just and the compassionate in relation to the 'other', without prejudice.

Prototype of missionary activity in Acts

In many respects, Luke is not only 'the first book' (Acts 1.1) chronologically of the Luke-Acts duology. Luke's portrayal of the ministry of Jesus and the disciples is prototypical of the ministry of the post-Easter Apostles, especially that of Paul and his colleagues. But the ministry in both books is not merely beneficial work that presents itself along the way. The ministry is missional. That is, disciples are 'sent' – commissioned – and expected to return to the commissioner with a report on their success (or failure).

In earlier discussions we encountered the Twelve and the seventy [-two]. In this discussion I will focus particularly on the dynamism in the missional texts related to each group respectively. I submit that the sequence of the two missional groups in Luke – the Twelve first and then the seventy [-two] – constitutes a prototypical pattern that finds fulfilment in the missional order in Acts: the missional preaching of Peter (with others) in chapters 2 to 12, followed by the missional preaching of Paul (with others) in the rest of Acts. The two are related to each other in both books, because the commissioner is one and the same for each of the two in each book.

Commission and return of the Twelve (Luke 9.1-10)

In exploring Luke 9.1-10 (as in 10.1-17 below) I note the prominence of power words in the mission narrative. How do these words relate to the conventional political and cultural terms of domination at the time of writing? Are they used in *contradistinction* to the prevailing words of Empire operating at the time? Or are they used in *conjunction* with the imperialist vocabulary?

The passage opens with Jesus calling the Twelve together to give them 'power' (*dynamis*) and 'authority' (*exousia*). The first of these two words denotes inherent energy or might that comes from *being* strong.

The inherent power of *dynamis* comes from the nature of the thing or the person thus endowed. The power of the Roman empire, for example, resides in the military legions, their weapons and resources, and in the political will to deploy those resources for imperial expansion and security. But *dynamis* power can reside in a person for good, so that the deeds flowing from such a person are miraculous and/or beneficial to human life. This latter fits Jesus' gift to the Twelve.

'Authority' (*exousia*) is also a power word, but with a different connotation. In this case the power is in the right and freedom to exercise the power to rule. Caesar in Rome had the *exousia* to order his army general to invade Palestine, to put down the rebellion, and ultimately to destroy Jerusalem and the Temple in the war of 66–70 CE.

In Luke 9.1, Jesus qualifies the two words, defines their use in his sending of the Twelve: the power and authority are 'over all demons and to cure diseases'. At face value, power in this case is meant for the human good. But as the text was appropriated along the way by Western missionaries within a colonialist mindset, the demons and even the diseases were often intertwined with cultural ideas and practices. Thus, sacred trees were chopped down, traditional shrines demolished and cultural practices disavowed as inferior at best, or evil at worst. The contra-definition and contra-appropriation of power words were, and still are, difficult for missionaries operating within a socio-political ideology of control.

Once Jesus granted 'power' and 'authority' to the Twelve, he 'sent' (*apostellō*) them out without designating territory or people groups, although the Galilee of Herod Antipas seems to be in view (vv. 7-9). The commissioned disciples (*apostoloi*, v. 10) had a dual assignment: to proclaim the kingdom of God and to heal. 'Kingdom of God', like the two power words above, was a politically charged term in the Roman-occupied provinces, such as Palestine. And like the other power words, this one runs the risk of being interpreted as the divine right of the kingdom-bringers to dominate people groups who do not share the same values as theirs.

But there is more to this text, two features in particular.

First, Jesus gives instructions to the commissioned disciples on how to go out into their mission. In a nutshell, they are to take nothing for their journey (v. 3a): no money, staff, bag, bread or coat. The notion of defensive weaponry is not remotely in the picture. They go out completely vulnerable. They will be at the mercy of their hosts. From them the missionaries will receive food and lodging, and whatever other necessities for life. From this description of mission 'strategy' we could not possibly draw the notion of domination in any way.

Traditionally Western missionaries have garnered their support from Western (home) sources, not from the receiving culture groups. That missionary practice of moving into 'foreign' cultures backed by Western money is a power play, one which does not follow the logic of the Lukan prototype. Jesus' 12 missionaries in this text have nothing. Their missionary posture is one of weakness and vulnerability.

If the receiving kin-groups do not receive the missionaries, then the missionaries simply leave that venue, after shaking the dust off their feet as a testimony against the villagers. That is, the missionaries take no responsibility for the well-being of the non-receptive villagers. On a positive note, however, the missionaries do bring a gift to their receptive host villagers: the gift of a new rule of life (kingdom of God), which casts out demons and heals diseases. It is a mystery how this sense of the text could have escaped colonialist-minded missionaries. The idea of *imposing* a Christian culture on a receiving culture is foreign to this text.

Second, it is a bit surprising to find the figure of 'Herod the ruler' at the end of this missionary narrative (vv. 7-9). His role in the narrative is one of sharp contrast. He stands out as one whose mission is violent, whose rule is oppressive and self-promoting. He had John the Baptist killed for bringing the truth to light. By contrast, these missionaries from Jesus bring a non-violent rule, a healing ministry and a totally vulnerable way of life: they open themselves to the good will – or bad – of their village hosts. Herein lies the prototype for mission in Acts, and for mission in generations for ever after.

The *pericopē* about the mission of the Twelve closes with their return to Jesus with a report of their experience: 'the [missionaries] told Jesus all they had done' (v. 10). In the absence of any reprimand in the narrative we may assume that the missionaries had followed their sending instructions. Thus ends the first missionary cycle in Luke. A similar literary pattern of sending, missionary practice, return and report holds for the mission of the seventy [-two] in Luke 10.

Commission and return of the seventy [-two] (Luke 10.1-17)

While Luke 10.1-17, about the sending of the seventy [-two], has a number of the features found in the former text about the sending of the Twelve, this one is by no means a repetition of the former. The 'sending' and 'return' are present here as before. The provisions for the journey are similar: no purse, no bag, no sandals, and greet no one on the road (v. 4). And the dependence on the good grace of the recipients is the same: 'eating and drinking whatever they provide' (v. 7). The 'deeds of power' (v. 13) are essentially the same also: healing the sick and bringing the kingdom of God near (v. 9). Again, the missionaries are to shake the dust off their feet against those who do not receive them (v. 11).

Now for the differences. It should be noted here that Luke draws on Mark's version of the sending of the Twelve (Mark 6.7-30) in composing *both* his sending stories, the Twelve and the seventy [-two]. Some parts from Mark are modified in the sending of the Twelve (Luke 9), while other parts are carried over into the sending of the seventy [-two] (Luke 10). In particular, the instruction about going out two by two comes over into the sending of the seventy [-two], and becomes prototypical of the mission of Paul and Barnabas (Acts 13–14), and Paul and Silas (Acts 15.40ff).

'Harvest' and 'labourers' are new to this narrative. The harvest may suggest the gathering of Israel, echoing Isaiah 27.12. If that is the echo here, then it is Israel as understood by the implied author of Luke-Acts: Israel that includes the Gentiles who believe in Jesus. The 'labourers' are the sent ones. Seventy [-two] are hardly 'few', at least not for Palestine. But in the context of the Gentile world mission described in Acts, seventy [-two] would not be too many. Interesting also is the appearance of three Gentile cities: Sodom, Tyre and Sidon (cf. Matt. 11.21-3). Judgement appears in this text as well. But it is not a judgement pronounced by the missionaries, or by the Church. It is the eschatological judgement before the tribunal of God. Presumably it is Jesus in the text who pronounces the woes on Chorazin, Bethsaida and Capernaum, not the missionaries (v. 13).

Too often colonialist missionaries have arrogated to themselves the prerogative of judgement that belongs to God alone. People who reject the missionaries and their message are not thereby subject to missionary domination, judgement or oppression. Their fate belongs to God, not to the seventy [-two].

The greeting the missionaries are expected to bring to their hosts is also significant. Whatever house they enter they are to say: 'Peace to this house'. The greeting could be construed as the ritual Jewish greeting, *shalōm*. But the peace is part of Jesus' instruction to the missionaries, not to be taken for granted. 'Peace' signifies human well-being: for good and not evil, 'for building … up and not for tearing … down' (2 Cor. 10.8).

The missionary cycle finishes, as it did for the Twelve, with the return of the seventy [-two] to Jesus and with their report to him. This time the report is more elaborate: 'the seventy [-two] returned with joy, saying, "Lord, in your name even the demons submit (*hupotassō*) to us!"' (v. 17). What is noteworthy about the term 'submit' – another power word – is not that the people submitted to the missionaries, but that the *demons* did. The distinction is important if we are to overcome the colonialist attitude that has so plagued the missionary enterprise of the last few centuries. Demons are by definition bad news, destructive to the human, cultural good. But a culture and its people are not the demons, and are therefore not subject to the 'power' of the missionaries.

Paul's missionary expansion among Gentiles

Just as the mission of the Twelve preceded the mission of the seventy [-two] in Luke, so in Acts the post-Easter mission of Peter precedes the mission of Paul. For the implied author of Luke-Acts, Peter's mission in Judaea is a necessary precursor to Paul's mission in the Gentile world.

Precursor I: one commission for both missions (Acts 1.8)

Both missions in Acts – Peter's and Paul's – rest on the *one* promissory commission of the *one* risen Jesus: 'you will receive power when the Holy Spirit has come upon you; and you will be my witnesses in Jerusalem, in all Judea and Samaria, and to the ends of the earth' (1.8). The 'power' (*dynamis*) here is the same as the power vouchsafed to the Twelve in Luke 9, except that here the disciples will receive it from the Holy Spirit. Unfortunately, some interpreters – consciously or unconsciously – have taken the power coming from the Holy Spirit to be inherently bigger and better than the power from Jesus. The Holy Spirit *extends* the power of Jesus beyond the venue of Palestine, but does not change or enhance the *character* of Jesus' power. It is still a power for goodness and peace and life. Those who receive power from the Holy Spirit become witnesses to Jesus, not witnesses to the Holy Spirit as though different from Jesus. They bear the stamp of Jesus' character and mission on their life in mission. That is equally true for Paul as for Peter, and for all who follow in their train.

Precursor II: Peter's mission as representative of the Twelve (Acts 1.15–12.17)

Peter, addressing the early community in Jerusalem, spoke on behalf of the Twelve. One of their number, Judas Iscariot, had betrayed Jesus and shortly thereafter died a horrible death, leaving the number at eleven.

Peter orchestrated a replacement for Judas by casting lots between two candidates. The lot fell to Matthias, bringing the Twelve back into play (1.15-26). Peter's mission that follows represents the Twelve, and lasts until the missionary takeover of Paul that represents the seventy [-two]. Paul, in this capacity in Acts, is aligned with Stephen and the *Hellenistai* (discussed in Chapter 4 above).

What was the character of Peter's mission under the power of the Holy Spirit? Briefly this: preaching the way of Jesus whom God raised from the dead (2.14-36; 3.12-26), and healing (3.1-10; 5.15-16).The scenario is the same as in the prototype in Luke 9: the word and work of Peter is received by some and rejected by others, but never imposed aggressively or oppressively. Rather, the Spirit-empowered Peter is brought to trial and imprisoned more than once by the authorities in the mission territory (4.1-22; 5.17-18; 12.3-11).

Peter remains in missionary mode until the end of chapter 12, has a vision for the inclusion of Gentiles (chapter 10), then drops out of the picture in chapters 13 and 14 when Paul enters. Peter reappears briefly again in chapter 15 for the Jerusalem Conference in support of Paul, after which he is heard from no more in Acts. Paul's westward mission takes over completely after the Jerusalem Conference, overshadowing the earlier mission of Peter.

But before leaving Peter's missionary precursor to Paul's more extensive work, it should not go unnoticed that King Herod (Agrippa I) comes in at the end of Peter's missionary sojourn in Acts, just as another King Herod (Antipas) came in at the end of the mission of the Twelve in Luke 9. Both Herods represent a worldly power in stark contrast to the power of God present in Peter, one of the twelve witnesses to Jesus. Herod of Luke 9 had John the Baptist beheaded. Herod of Acts 12 'had James, the brother of John, killed with the sword' (12.2). Such a dastardly act of villainy does not miss the all-seeing eye of God. Divine judgement falls swiftly on the self-glorying Herod of Acts 12: 'an angel of the Lord struck him down, and he was eaten by worms' (12.23). Such is the picture of the justice of God at work in Acts: Peter is miraculously delivered while Herod is ignominiously destroyed. The hands of the missionary are clean on all counts.

Something is missing

Before taking up the subject of Paul's call and mission, however, notice should be given about the selective character of Acts' depiction of the early missionary movement. It begins with Peter's preaching and healing in Jerusalem and environs, moves northward because of the persecution that broke out over Stephen's testimony (6.8–8.2), establishes a new centre in Antioch of Syria, and moves west from there. Acts gives no account of Paul's travels eastward into Arabia (Gal. 1.17; 2 Cor. 11.32-3), and no indication of other missionaries taking the gospel of Jesus to Egypt or Babylonia or other points eastward. We know now that an early community did exist in Egypt, and probably also in south India. Acts focuses strictly on the mission to the west. This missionary schema in Acts has doubtless shaped the history of interpretation within dominant Western Christianity. And the longer the history, it seems, the greater the conviction of superiority of the dominant West down to the present time.

Attention should be drawn as well to the Western interpretation of 'three missionary journeys of Paul' as successively expanding. Acts does not list three journeys as such, as though Paul had strategically planned three successive missions into Gentile territory and culture. Granted, there is a kind of cyclical pattern to his various travels here and there: he returns to base (Antioch/Jerusalem) after his itinerant preaching foray, reports and then goes out again. The pattern echoes the mission of the Twelve and seventy [-two] in Luke: they go out and then return to Jesus with a report. Paul and his companion return to the sending church.

Early missionary extension out of Antioch, culminating in the decision of the Jerusalem Conference (Acts 13.1–14.28)

I cannot in this space go into the details of the missionary activity depicted in these two chapters (readers should familiarize themselves with the text). Suffice it merely to draw attention to points of connection with the sending of the seventy [-two] in Luke 10, and then points of extension beyond the Lukan prototype.

1. The 'sending' authority now rests with the Holy Spirit on the one hand and the church at Antioch in Syria on the other (13.1-4). The church at Antioch does not consult with any member of the Jerusalem group about the mission. Like the sending of the seventy [-two] in Luke 10, the sending of Paul and Barnabas occurs independently of the sanction of the Jerusalem group, Peter and/or the Twelve.
2. Upon completion of the assigned work, the missionaries return to the sending base, the church at Antioch, and give a report: 'they called the church together and related all that God had done with them, and how he had opened a door of faith for the Gentiles' (14.26-7).

3. The missionary work consisted in preaching the good news about the grace of God in raising Jesus (13.23-39; 14.15), and in healing (14.8-10). Note, there is nothing in these chapters about casting out demons, as such. Other gods come into play in the narrative. But there is no explicit indication that the missionaries equated the gods of the peoples with demons. Rather, they considered the idols of the gods 'worthless things', and invited the worshippers to turn from them to 'the living God' (14.15). This is a far cry from recklessly smashing idols and casting aspersion on the worshippers.

4. One of the instructions to the seventy [-two] in Luke 10 was that they go out two by two. In these chapters in Acts, the twosome is consistently highlighted: Paul and Barnabas are together from beginning to end in the itinerant activity.

5. The notion of reception and rejection is also sharply focused in Acts 13 and 14. With the acceptance of the two missionaries and their message, good will and blessing fall to the recipients. By contrast, when people of a village or city rejected the emissaries, sometimes persecuting them severely, the two missionaries simply 'shook the dust off their feet in protest against them' (13.51). One can hear a loud echo of the Lukan instruction from Jesus. This is not retaliation, but a non-violent gesture of disapproval towards their belligerent rejection of 'good news'.

Points of extension, or difference, also come through.

1. In Cyprus, Paul and Barnabas encounter a Jewish magician, Elymas, also called a 'false prophet', who opposed the missionaries and tried to turn the proconsul away from the faith. For this insolence the magician was afflicted with blindness 'for a while'. Justification for this affliction on his person is that he is a 'son of the devil, enemy of righteousness, full of deceit and villainy … making crooked the straight paths of the Lord' (13.6-11).

   There is nothing comparable to this retaliatory action in the ministry of Jesus in Luke (or in the other Gospels). In this case, judgement falls on the offender there and then, and that in accordance with the word of the missionaries. Such a negative 'miracle' at the hands of Paul and Barnabas provides – all too easily – scriptural ground for punishing opponents of the missionary message. One shudders to think how this text might be used in the hands of power brokers in some Christian churches.

2. When the two missionaries healed the cripple at Lystra, the people acclaimed them as gods, Zeus and Hermes, incarnate (14.8-17). The

situation provides the opportunity to proclaim One God to the polytheistic Gentiles of the town. This one God bears witness to all, even to idolatrous Gentiles, 'doing good – giving you rains from heaven and fruitful seasons, and filling you with food and your hearts with joy'. Thus, this God is not only the 'living God', but also the life-giving God. How then could his ambassadors hold a dominant, imposing attitude?

3. In Antioch of Pisidia Paul was invited to preach in the synagogue on one Sabbath and then another. A number of Jewish people and converts to Judaism accepted the message, believing in Jesus. On the second Sabbath a great crowd came out to hear Paul. Jewish leaders became jealous and contradicted Paul, rejecting the message of Jesus resurrected. With that rejection, according to Paul and Barnabas, they have judged themselves 'unworthy of eternal life'. The Jewish rejection provides the occasion for a most unlikely declaration: 'we are now turning to the Gentiles' (*ethne* = nations, Acts 13.46). Unlikely because the two missionaries are Jewish, with all the Israelite tradition of divine election and special privilege for one nation over the many behind them. Now 'the many' are 'destined for eternal life' through faith in Jesus. As one might expect, the Gentiles in the audience 'were glad and praised the word of the Lord; as many as had been destined for eternal life became believers' (13.48). This marks a significant extension beyond the prototype of the mission of the seventy [-two] in Luke 10.

And it also triggers a critical moment in the development of the primitive community of Jesus: a call for a conference in Jerusalem to determine how 'the many' Gentiles are to be incorporated into the new people of God (Acts 15; cf. Gal. 2.1-10). Do the traditional Jewish marks of inclusion hold for believing Gentiles? A number of markers were set aside, probably because adult Gentiles were averse to submitting to them. Circumcision, a deeply rooted mark of the covenant, was repugnant to adult Gentile males. That mark was set aside. Sabbath-keeping, another notable mark of the covenant in the first century, simply does not come into focus in Acts 15. As noted in Chapter 5 above, the only requirements imposed on Gentile believers were that they abstain from idol-meat and from sexual immorality, and that they observe some food regulations. Paul, as we have found in his letters, remembers the conference differently: '[the Jerusalem leaders] asked only one thing, that we remember the poor, which was actually what I was eager to do' (Gal. 2.10; cf. 1 Cor. 10.25).

The question of how much to impose on new believers is ever present in missional work. Even when religious groups invoke what 'seemed good to the Holy Spirit and to us', the result is usually an imposition of doctrine and practice anchored in a particular religious tradition. It may or may not be beneficial for the believers in another culture.

Post-conference forays extending to Macedonia/Greece and returning to Jerusalem (Acts 15.36–21.16)

Paul's post-conference missionary forays recorded in Acts 15.36–21.16 are thickly textured with many narrative details. A full exploration of the text would be impossible here. At the same time, it is important to recognize this large section of text as missionary in nature, and notoriously subjected to an interpretation of conquest.

The first order of business is to determine whether the basic parameters of the prototype in Luke 10 operate here in Paul's extension of missionary activity westward into Macedonia and Greece. To say that Paul's mission 'moved forward into Europe' is at best a misnomer, and at worst an exhibition of a colonialist attitude imposed on the text. Europe as we know it did not exist at the time.

The basic parameters of mission of the Luke 10 prototype are present in various settings in this larger mission of Paul: a *pair* of missionaries, *proclamation* of the kingdom (or kingship) of God in Jesus, *healing* the sick, *casting out demons*, and the *reception–rejection* pattern, with the rejection by Jewish people being the catalyst for going on to the Gentiles.

Paul and Silas – not Barnabas – are the pair of missionaries in this round. Paul had a disagreement with Barnabas over the reliability of John Mark, so Paul chose Silas as his companion instead in the ensuing mission (15.36-40).

The proclamation of the kingdom of God met with no small resistance, particularly at Thessalonica in Macedonia. An accusation was brought against Paul and Silas and their friends that they were 'turning the world upside-down' and 'acting contrary to the decrees of the emperor, saying that there is another king named Jesus' (17.4-9). Despite the political risk of using the terms 'king' and 'kingdom', Paul continued to use them in his preaching. Their counter-imperialist implication caught the attention of some opponents in Paul's audience. 'Turning the world upside-down' is doubtless an exaggeration on the lips of the accusers. Nevertheless, 'king' (Messiah) and 'kingdom' are provocative, begging the question about the emperor's right to rule the world as he does from his throne in Rome.

Paul's healing ministry also continues in fulfilment of the earlier prototype in Luke 10. But it continues in some very extraordinary ways, one might say magical ways. Handkerchiefs and aprons that touched Paul's skin were brought to the sick and they were healed (19.11). Apparently, healing in the name of Jesus can take more than one form. Medical science would surely disapprove of such way-out methods of healing. But if the end is for the human good, why insist on the supremacy of the scientific method? If native medicine is effective, why declare it unacceptable? The heart of the matter is that the 'good news' in Christian mission is healing news, not hurtful news.

Casting out demons also continues in Paul's mission. One case sparks particular interest. It happened as a result of a night-vision Paul had during his stay at Troas. In the vision he saw and heard a man of Macedonia pleading with him: 'Come over and help us.' This experience convinced Paul that God was calling him to 'proclaim the good news' to the people of Macedonia (16.9-10). Two words stand together in this text: 'help' (*boetheō*) and 'proclaim good news' (*euanglizō*). Both words have been interpreted through colonialist lenses along the way. The help has often been understood as Western Christian help, which includes all kinds of cultural trappings, including Western hymns and forms of worship. Similarly, proclaiming good news all too often was deemed 'good' because it bore the marks of the dominant Western patterns of life and thought and theology. If a culture is afflicted with demons, however, then it would *help* to cast them out. Demons are by definition destructive to the human good. It remains for readers of the text to judge whether Paul was doing good when he cast the demon out of the 'slave-girl' in Philippi.

Two women stand side by side in the Philippi narrative (16.11-18), the 'slave-girl' (*paidiske*) and Lydia. The 'slave-girl' has no other name in the narrative beyond this social designation. The other woman has a name, Lydia, and a trade, dealing in purple cloth. She is a worshipper of God. Both her worship and her work are approved in the story. A fair inference is that the God she was worshipping was the God of Israel, not a local god of the people. Lydia is a receptive host to the missionaries, invites Paul and Silas to stay at her house, and submits to their baptism.

By contrast the nameless 'slave-girl' has a 'spirit of divination' that enabled her to see beyond the surface and beyond the present. She could tell fortunes. Her owners used her power to make money for themselves. But was her spirit evil or good? She followed Paul and Silas and shouted out: 'These men are slaves of the Most High God, who proclaim to you a way of salvation' (16.17). This appears to be a rather good and true description of the missionaries and their message. But Paul was 'very much annoyed' because she followed him and kept on shouting the same thing. So he turned and ordered the 'demon' to come out of her.

And it did that very hour. She was still a slave, but now a worthless one to her owners. One can only guess what her fate might have been. The text is silent on the matter.

The owners of the girl had Paul and Silas thrown in prison, because they had disrupted their lucrative business coming from their slave. Lydia returns at the end of the long prison story (16.40), but the 'slave-girl' not at all. Her voice is silenced by the Acts narrator, and her lot in life thereafter banished to literary oblivion. One is left wondering about the 'help' Paul and his companions brought to this nameless girl in Macedonia. It is clear they divested her owners of their means of making money. But is it true to the text to say that Paul objected to the way her owners were using her, and thus he cast out the 'spirit of divination'? The textual fact is that Paul was 'very much annoyed' at her for following him and telling everyone repeatedly about their mission.

Of the several surprises throughout the missionary narrative, none is more surprising than the story of Paul's circumcising young Timothy (16.1-3). The Jerusalem Conference had settled that question to everyone's satisfaction, it seems. Why on earth would Paul then circumcise Timothy? His Jewish mother had not done so at eight days, and presumably the synagogue authorities had not insisted on it, perhaps because his father was Greek. Paul's action in doing so could set a precedent for all Greek converts to the new community of Jesus Messiah.

The motive given in Acts is several-fold: because Paul wanted Timothy to accompany him; because Jewish leaders would expect Timothy to be circumcised; because his father was Greek. The reasons make no sense, especially the last one, in light of the recent decision coming out of Jerusalem. Paul could refer to the decision given in writing: circumcision is not required of Greek believers in Jesus the Christ.

Paul's move appears tactical, if not political. The Jewish leaders, knowing Timothy's father was Greek, might call for an inspection of Timothy. By circumcising Timothy in advance of his travels, Paul would spare himself and Timothy an inquisition, and perhaps punishment, from the synagogue authorities. Timothy could enter the synagogues with Paul unchallenged.

When Paul reached Corinth, he had the same reception–rejection experience. For the first time we have some indication of what shaking the dust from oneself meant to those who did so. The record shows that when some at Corinth 'opposed and reviled [Paul], in protest he shook the dust from his clothes' (18.6a). The echo is audible, with slight variation from the instruction of Jesus in Luke 10.11. But in the Acts text the sign is accompanied by a descriptive word: 'Your blood be on your own heads! I am innocent' (18.6a). Paul takes no responsibility for what might befall them in the future. Furthermore, this opposition from the

Jewish side provides Paul the opportunity to say: 'From now on I will go to the Gentiles' (18.6b; cf. 13.46).

Finally, we recognize Paul's two returns to base within the post-conference mission narrative. He returned at the end of chapter 18 and again at the beginning of chapter 21. Both times Paul returns to Jerusalem, not Antioch. On his last return he is arrested, unable to go out again via Antioch as he had done after his return at the end of chapter 18 (cf. 18.22-3). But the two circles out and back should not be construed as Paul's second and third missionary journeys, as though he was engaged in an ever-widening acquisition of Gentile territory and people. Paul stays with people in their homes, in one place for 18 months (18.11), in another for two years (19.10).

Rather than a takeover of lands and peoples, the return to Jerusalem from mission among Gentiles might best be taken as Paul's symbolic ingathering of believing Gentiles into covenant relationship with Israel through Paul's agency in the name of Jesus, Messiah of God. Paul's return to Jerusalem was not a political move in the conventional sense, but a theological one, I suggest. Paul did not take the Gentiles out of their culture by his return to Jerusalem – unlike the imperialist Babylonians who took the Judaeans captive into Babylonia in 597–87 BCE. Paul left them in their social and cultural place with assurance that their eternal salvation was secure in communion with Jesus Christ and his people.

Further reading

To become familiar with a postcolonial way of reading biblical texts, consult R. S. Sugirtharajah, 'A brief memorandum on postcolonialism and biblical studies', *Journal for the Study of the New Testament* 73 (1999), 3–5; and his *Postcolonial Reconfigurations* (2003); see also Sugirtharajah's collection of essays in *The Postcolonial Bible* (1998), and Broadbent *et al.*'s review, '"*The Postcolonial Bible*": Four Reviews', *Journal for the Study of the New Testament* 74 (1999), pp. 113–21. Michael Prior's book focuses on the ideology and interpretation of 'land': *The Bible and Colonialism: A Moral Critique* (1997); see also Pablo Richard, 'The hermeneutics of liberation: a hermeneutics of the spirit' (1995), pp. 263–80.

Review questions

1. What is a postcolonial interpretation?
2. How important is it to acknowledge one's enculturated ideas,

beliefs and practices?

3. What are the implications of Jesus' instructions for the mission of the Twelve and the seventy [-two] in Luke?

4. What does the symbolic gesture of 'shaking the dust off your feet' signify?

5. How do the missions of Peter and Paul in Acts correspond to the missions of the Twelve and the seventy [-two] in Luke?

6. What does it mean to 'read against the grain'? Illustrate with reference to the 'slave-girl' in Acts 16.1-18.

8

Feminist praxis: 'both men and women'

This chapter follows up on the previous one. Both chapters exemplify a political interpretation concerning rulers and ruled. Moreover, the self-appropriation for doing a postcolonial reading of Luke-Acts holds true for this chapter on a feminist reading. The question is the same: Who is in a position to interpret the texture of Luke-Acts using a feminist-praxis approach? That approach springs from the efforts of women scholars to become free from male domination, to act as equals with men in every aspect of social, economic, religious and political life. The answer to the question should be obvious: women engaged in the struggle for freedom are the ones to interpret the texts that have been used against them.

Here I am, a white male descendant of 'Eurocentric malestream scholarship' (Schüssler Fiorenza, *Rhetoric and Ethic* (1999), 46–7) presuming to interpret Luke-Acts in a way that reflects the concerns of women in the present time. Yet I do not want to be excluded from feminist scholarly enterprise. I have read the works of feminist biblical scholars, have learned so much from them, and am persuaded that their cause is just. I want to read *along with* women interpreters, not merely as listener, but as sympathetic participant. I have no illusions that my feminist reading of Luke-Acts will be completely free of traditional male overtones. To the extent that these are present they are unintentional.

Suspicion

One of the principles in a hermeneutics of liberation, of which feminist interpretation is a part, is an attitude and practice of suspicion. Scripture texts that deal with socially marginalized people – slaves, peasants, non-literate, children, the sick, women – should be viewed as dangerous to the health of women. The texts come out of a patriarchal, agrarian culture in which an ideology of hierarchy was the order of the day, with elitist males in positions of power. Furthermore, the endless round of commentaries on the texts through successive centuries has reinforced the patriarchal hierarchy, casting it into a divinely ordained order of society.

A hermeneutics of suspicion subverts long-standing traditional interpretations that have tended to portray the female gender as occupying a secondary, or subservient role. Positively, a feminist picture of the biblical God as deliverer of the enslaved, the marginalized, the oppressed becomes the anvil on which a feminist interpretation is hammered out. Feminist biblical scholars from the 1970s onward have called upon the tested and tried tools of biblical criticism, especially historical criticism, to demonstrate the viability of feminist interpretive projects in biblical and theological studies.

Deconstruction and reconstruction

The work of the French philosopher Jacques Derrida, from his earliest writings of the 1960s until his death on 8 October 2004, challenged the traditional interpretation of texts significantly. His theory is captured particularly in the word 'deconstruction'. Derrida's theory is provocative, calling into question the self-evident, logical, non-judgemental character of the myriad pairs of opposites by which we construct social reality. We speak of good and bad, rational and irrational, fact and fiction, right and wrong. The dichotomies appear in literature, speech, gestures, policy-making, etc. Language especially carries the structures by which people in society live their daily lives. But the dichotomies, like the language in which they appear, are *socially* constructed. They are not eternally fixed forms. That means they are subject to deconstruction. And deconstruction in turn should lead to authenticity and equality in human relationships.

Not only are there pairs of opposites in social texture, but one of the pairs is privileged over the other. Hence we have male and female, light and darkness, good and evil, etc. Notice that the subtitle of this chapter is 'both men and women'. The phrase appears five times in that form in Acts (2.18; 5.14; 8.3, 12; 22.4). It would be strange indeed to encounter one instance (even in the NRSV that touts gender inclusiveness) of 'both female and male'. Male is privileged by its initial position in the phrase.

The structure of the language reflects the social reality within which the language operates. Luke-Acts was written within a predominantly patriarchal and imperialist social reality, as were all other writings of the New Testament. Yet not all writings exhibit the same hierarchal patriarchy. For example, when Mark and Luke narrate the story of the feeding of the five thousand, they say simply that there were five thousand *men* (Mark 6.44; Luke 9.14). The total absence of women from the narrative crowd of five thousand hungry people is deafening by the silence in the text. Were women really not present? Or were they present but not hungry? Or were they present and hungry but unimportant as compared to the hunger of the men? Matthew seems to have deconstructed the silence/absence to a point, but then reconstructs the text in classic patriarchal fashion to read: 'those who ate were about five thousand men, *besides women and children*' (Matt. 14.21, italics mine). Women and children are secondary to men. They literally don't count among the five thousand hungry men. (One wonders what the total number would be if women and children were counted!) Thus, Matthew's kind of deconstruction and reconstruction only adds insult to injury, making the marginalized unapologetically visible as marginalized. The patriarchal and imperial structure is reinforced in Matthew.

Texts like that of the feeding of five thousand *men* should not be overlooked in any feminist search for the origins of the liberating message of Jesus in the Gospels. It is certainly appropriate to focus on those women disciples who made a contribution to the Jesus movement, and to take our cue for women's roles from them. But the New Testament literature is mixed. There are signs galore of women cast in a secondary, subservient role to men. And texts that exhibit that condition demand a judgement from the present-day women and men who promote the liberating gospel of Jesus the Christ. Deconstruction of the language of the texts, using the tools of historical-critical analysis, is a move towards making the news of Jesus *good* news. Reconstruction follows deconstruction. It must, otherwise the labour of deconstruction is in vain. Reconstruction calls for a reformulation of the text-language of liberation from oppression, and with that the reconstitution of the social texture and institutions within which children and women and men live together.

The presence of women in the narrative

Recently the Dean of a new Christian university in Canada called attention to the ratio of female to male members of faculty. The statistics did not speak well for the university's hiring practice. The ratio of males to females was 2.1. Gender imbalance like this in institutions of higher learning is unacceptable by the canons of twenty-first-century

Table 8.1

Mark (43 pages of text)		Matthew (83 pages of text)		Luke (91 pages of text)	
Woman =	2	Woman =	10	Woman =	18
Women =	6	Women =	6	Women =	12
Total =	8	Total =	16	Total =	30
Man =	49	Man =	66	Man =	88
Men =	3	Men =	10	Men =	10
Total =	52	Total =	76	Total =	98

enlightenment. While simple statistics like these do not account for all factors, they do signal a need for administrators to evaluate the situation.

Gender statistics for Luke-Acts likewise do not tell the whole story. At the same time, they can assist in evaluating the extent to which New Testament writers were part of the social matrix of the imperialist system that privileged men over women.

The implied author of Luke is often viewed as the evangelist most concerned about the place of women in the new community of Jesus the Christ. And when gender words are tabulated and compared to their occurrence in the other Synoptic Gospels, the writer of Luke does indeed come across as someone more concerned about the role of women in the community of Jesus and in society. Using the gender terms 'woman'/'women' and 'man'/'men', Table 8.1 compares the ratios between women and men and between the three Synoptic Gospels.

The ratio of men to women in the totals for the three columns suggests that, of the three, Luke is more disposed to having women present in the narrative than either of the other two: 3:2:1, against Matthew's 4:7:1 or Mark's 6:5:1. Luke-Acts overall, however, shows 'man/men' to 'woman/women' at 4:8:1. Perhaps little is gained by tallying the number of times gender terms appear in a narrative. The exercise does tend to confirm the suspicion that Luke-Acts has not risen far above the Graeco-Roman imperialist worldview that privileges the male over the female in society. Luke-Acts in the end is not about the emancipation of women understood in present-day categories.

There are women in Luke-Acts who could serve as role models for the present-day Church and world. And feminist interpreters have worked diligently to peel back layers of malestream interpretations that have kept them in the shadows – if not in the closets – of male leadership in the Church. Yet even when the honourable women of

Luke-Acts are revealed, their presence (with a few exceptions) is scarcely as prominent as their male counterparts. In short, objectionable as it feels today, there is not in Luke-Acts an outright emancipation of women from their diminished gendered status within the pervasive ideology of Mediterranean culture. But there is promise in Luke-Acts, especially in the attitude and action of the Lukan Jesus toward women: promise of equal status between women and men in all aspects of socio-cultural and churchly life and work. 'Both men and women' in Acts promises equality, promises a time and place in history when the terms will be interchangeable in sentence structure: 'both women and men', equally human, equally gifted and educated, equally in Christ and in ministry. I submit that that time and place has come. (See Gal. 3.28 and Schüssler Fiorenza (1999), 149–73.)

Absentees

In Luke-Acts women are sometimes missing from narratives by explicit exclusion, or implicitly absent from narrative settings by remaining unidentified. We shall take up several examples of both of these conditions.

Absent from the five thousand (Luke 9.10-17 // Mark 6.31-44; Matt. 14.13-21)

I take it that the implied author of Luke used Mark as his source for the miracle story of the feeding of the multitude. But he does not slavishly follow the sequence of events in his source, or even the wording in his source.

For example, the Markan narrator says of Jesus and the crowd, 'he had compassion for them, because they were like sheep without a shepherd; and he began to teach them many things' (6.34). The Lukan redactor reworks the material thus: 'he welcomed them, and spoke to them about the kingdom of God, and healed those who needed to be cured' (9.11). Mark's seating arrangement of the crowd 'in groups of hundreds and of fifties' (6.40) must have looked strange to the Lukan redactor, so he changes it to read, 'in groups of about fifty each' (9.14). Also changed in Luke is the position of the comment about the number five thousand. Mark puts the comment at the end of the miracle (6.44), whereas Luke has it in the middle, while the disciples are debating about the lack of bread (9.14). One final example, and an important one, illustrates the freedom of the Lukan redactor to change Mark's terms.

Throughout Mark's story the narrator refers consistently to Jesus' assistants in the miracle event as 'his disciples' (6.35, 41). Luke qualifies Mark's 'disciples' to read 'the twelve' – meaning the twelve *men* Jesus chose, whose names are on record in Luke 6. Nor is this surprising. The implied author of Luke-Acts views 'the Twelve' as the symbolic outcome of the heritage enshrined in the twelve sons of Jacob-Israel chosen by God for the salvation of the world.

The point to this examination of Luke's way of working with the material of his source is to ask why the Lukan redactor was not disturbed by Mark's total exclusion of women from the large crowd of Jesus' followers who needed bread. He could just as easily have changed Mark's 'five thousand men' (*pentakischilioi andres*) to 'more than five thousand people' (*pleious pentakischilioi laoi*), and thus have included children and women. Moreover, if the implied author of Luke-Acts has genuine concern for including women wherever possible, for giving them a place of honour equal with men, he missed a golden opportunity to do so in this text. Matthew at least acknowledged their presence at the scene, if only in a backhanded way (14.21).

The Syrophoenician woman missing (see Mark 7.24-30)

An argument from silence is seldom persuasive. I enter it here in any case. Even though the Lukan redactor draws on Mark for material from the Jesus tradition, he leaves out a story that could fit well into his schema of the gospel moving from the people of Israel to the peoples of the Gentile world. In Mark 7 Jesus leaves the environs of Lower Galilee to go to Tyre, there to withdraw from the crowds. But his reputation as healer had preceded him, so a woman finds him and begs him to heal her daughter who has an 'unclean spirit'. Jesus tells the woman: 'Let the children be fed first, for it is not fair to take the children's food and throw it to the dogs' (7.27). But she pleads: 'Sir, even the dogs under the table eat the children's crumbs' (7.28). Upon hearing her words Jesus heals the woman's daughter.

Why the Lukan redactor omitted the miracle story is puzzling. One would think the story would serve the purpose of the two-part work that has the gospel move beyond the borders of Palestine into the Gentile world. Furthermore, if the redactor is interested in women in need of recognition here is a perfect example. But this woman and her daughter are missing from Luke. Questions about the omission remain. Is the story missing from Luke because Jesus used the word 'dogs' to refer to Gentiles? Is it missing because the Gentile mission was not in force until after the resurrection? Or is it missing because this

Syrophoenician *woman* was bold enough to persuade Jesus to grant her request? It is interesting that other women in Luke who come to Jesus for healing, or for wisdom, do not approach him as the Syrophoenician woman did, insisting that he grant her wish. But Luke does have the Markan story of the woman suffering from haemorrhages for 12 years. She simply touched the hem of Jesus' garment in secret. Jesus felt the power go out of him, and exposed the woman's identity: 'When the woman saw that she could not remain *hidden*, she came trembling.' This story from Mark is included, but the one about the forceful Gentile woman is missing. And that is as far as one dare go in the absence of more concrete textual evidence.

More than twelve disciples

Twelve males from among others

Often the Gospels point to Jesus' disciples as a group without gender or number identity. True, the Greek word for 'disciples' (*hoi mathetai*) is grammatically masculine, but inclusive unless otherwise stipulated. The group could be made up of women and men under the general rubric 'disciples'. Disciples are learners. They learn the wisdom of the teacher by being *with* the teacher in all the situations of his life, watching his actions and listening to his words, and doing what the master does. Usually a master-teacher could have with him only so many disciples. If the group were too large the learning would be less effective. Mark makes clear that Jesus chose 12 in particular, whom he also called 'apostles' (sent ones), and then Mark gives the names of the 12 chosen ones. They are definitely all males (3.14-19). And Luke follows Mark, listing their male names (Luke 6.13-16).

Moreover, it is clear from Mark, followed by Luke (and also Matthew), that Jesus deliberately selected 12 males as the *inner circle* of disciples that he would call 'apostles'. The status of 'the twelve apostles' became firmly fixed in the primitive Church's tradition, so much so that Paul had to defend his post-Easter apostleship more than once (see 1 Cor. 9.2-3; Gal. 1.1; 2.8; Rom. 1.5). Luke-Acts makes no attempt to play down the distinctive priority of the Twelve and their male gender.

That being said, it is striking how Luke, as compared to Mark, describes the appointment of the Twelve. Mark simply says: '[Jesus] appointed twelve, whom he also named apostles, to be with him, and to be sent out to proclaim the message, and to have authority to cast out demons' (3.14-16). Luke, on the other hand, makes clear that the

Twelve were appointed from among a larger group of disciples: 'he called his disciples and chose twelve of them, whom he also named apostles' (6.13). The NRSV fails to capture the significance of the selection of twelve *from among* others in the larger group of disciples. The phrase (*ap' autōn*) means clearly 'from them'; that is, from the other disciples around Jesus. Of course, this merely indicates that there were more than 12 disciples with Jesus in Galilee. It does not prove that some of them were women.

However, other texts in Luke and Acts make explicit reference to women disciples who were with Jesus in his ministry in Galilee, and who travelled with him to Jerusalem. On one of Jesus' preaching tours through the cities and villages of Galilee, 'the twelve were with him, as well as some women who had been cured of evil spirits and infirmities' (8.1-2). By being 'with him' the followers learned the way of Jesus, learned his words and watched his action. In addition to the Twelve, the only other disciples travelling with Jesus on this trip were some women. And these same women appear again in Jerusalem as having travelled with Jesus. They witnessed the crucifixion, and are specifically mentioned as the ones watching as Jesus died: 'all his acquaintances, including the women who had followed him from Galilee, stood at a distance, watching these things' (23.49). The same women 'who had come from Galilee' followed Joseph of Arimathea to the tomb and saw how the body was laid. Then they 'returned and prepared spices and ointments' and rested on the Sabbath day (23.55-6). 'Returned' to what place? Presumably to the place where they were staying in Jerusalem, and to the people with whom they were staying. But where was that? And who were the people?

Answers come from the narrative about the resurrection morning, the first day of the week. The women come back to the tomb with the spices and perfumes they have prepared, and they find the stone rolled away and the body gone. They are perplexed and terrified. Then two angelic figures appear to them with a message. '"Remember how he told you, while he was still in Galilee, that the Son of Man must be handed over to sinners, and be crucified, and on the third day rise again." Then they remembered his words' (24.5-8). For the women to remember these particular words meant that they, along with the Twelve, were privy to Jesus' teaching concerning his suffering, death and resurrection. They were truly disciples of Jesus during his ministry in Galilee.

After this experience beside the tomb they returned and 'told all this to the eleven and to all the rest' (24.9). Again the word 'returned' appears. But this time the 'return' is more specific. They 'returned' to the eleven and the rest. In other words, these women disciples from

Galilee were part of a larger group of disciples of Jesus who came to Jerusalem with Jesus. Among the number of unnamed women three seem to belong to an inner circle, judging by the mention of their names in particular: 'Mary Magdalene, Joanna, Mary the mother of James, and the other women'. These women disciples from Galilee 'told this to the apostles' (24.10).

Another question comes to the fore immediately. Does 'apostles' here refer only to the eleven? It seems unlikely. Just a few verses before 24.10 the women returned from their experience at the tomb to 'the eleven and to all the rest'. It is hard to imagine the women telling their story to the eleven and not to the rest. Moreover, the eleven and the rest appear to be called 'apostles' in 24.10.

All this is to say that while the redactor of Luke clearly highlights a particular group of disciples as 'the Twelve', and reveals their maleness by stating their names, he does not restrict discipleship or apostleship to these 12 men. As we shall see shortly, the presence of women in the disciple-community of Jesus carries over into the early post-Easter community reflected in the early part of Acts.

Repeatedly, the male-dominated Church of later generations used the male membership of the inner circle of Jesus' 12 disciples to perpetuate exclusive male leadership in the ministry of word and sacrament. Only recently have some Protestant denominations broken with the tradition and ordained gifted, educated women to senior leadership roles in congregations.

My understanding of the historical Jesus' choice of 12 *men* from the larger group of male and female disciples was *not* to exclude women from leadership roles for ever after. It was rather to symbolize Israel's 12 *sons* reconstituted, Israel restored. If Jesus' aim was to signal *that* vision to his contemporaries in Palestine, then it would have been counterproductive to select an equal number of women and men to make up 'the Twelve'. And the implied author of Luke-Acts knows that as well as anyone. But Luke-Acts also knows that the new Israel includes Gentiles on a par with Judaeans – a breakthrough of immense proportion! With that equalizing breakthrough come others as well, not least the equalizing baptism of 'both men and women' (Acts 8.12).

Seventy [-two] others unidentified (10.1-20)

The gender composition of the seventy [-two] is not given in the text. They are simply called 'others' (10.1). That is, others of Jesus' disciples appointed for a mission of healing and preaching the kingdom of

God. We have discovered already the male–female composition of Jesus' followers in Galilee and Jerusalem. Given that discovery, it would be stretching credulity to think that the redactor of Luke has in mind males only for the larger group of seventy-two 'others'. Furthermore, if our earlier judgement is correct, that the seventy [-two] of Luke are prototypical of the mission of Paul and his companions in Acts, then we can reasonably infer that women were among the seventy [-two] of Luke 10. Reasonably, because the narrator of Paul's missionary activity in Acts specifically names women who joined Paul in his missionary work: Lydia (16.14-15), Damaris (17.34) and Priscilla (18.18, 26).

The whole multitude of disciples (Luke 19.37)

One of the very memorable events narrated in all four Gospels is that of Jesus' entry into Jerusalem on the back of a young donkey while people spread their cloaks (Luke) or branches (Mark and Matthew) on the road before him, shouting messianic praises to God. While all four Gospels speak of 'a crowd' involved in the festive activity, only Luke has 'the whole multitude of the **disciples**' praising 'joyfully with a loud voice for all the deeds of power that they had seen, saying, "Blessed is the king who comes in the name of the Lord! Peace in heaven, and glory in the highest heaven!"' (19.37-8).

Apparently the Lukan redactor cannot understand how Mark's unqualified multitude of Jerusalemites would suddenly burst into a song of praise for this Galilean peasant-figure on a donkey. Those who would praise God with such a song would be those who had known Jesus intimately, those who had been with him on the journey from Galilee. Hence the multitude of *disciples*. A 'multitude' in Lukan perspective would not require thousands. The 120 believers of Acts 1.15 constitute a 'crowd' (*ochlos*). Indeed, these 120 believers may be the very ones that the redactor of Luke has in view as the singing disciples at Jesus' jubilant entry into Jerusalem.

Now the question is: What was the gender-composition of the 'multitude of disciples' celebrating Jesus' entry into the Holy City? We have found already that an undesignated number of women had travelled with Jesus from Galilee to Jerusalem, witnessed his crucifixion, heard the resurrection message, and proclaimed the good news to the apostles (Luke 23.49, 55; 24.10). Of all the people that would have been in the 'whole multitude of disciples' following Jesus on a donkey, surely these women would have been there singing and celebrating with the rest.

There is one more important setting of Jesus' time in Jerusalem from which women have been traditionally excluded.

Participants at the Last Supper

The Church, with the help of the artist Leonardo da Vinci among others, established firmly the Markan tradition that Jesus ate his last Passover meal exclusively in the company of his 12 male disciples (Mark 14.17; Matt. 26.20). Luke's more inclusive rendering of the event has gone virtually unnoticed. It has been assumed that Luke's participants, called interchangeably 'apostles' (22.14) and 'disciples' (22.11, 39), must mean the Twelve of Mark's account. But that assumption is flawed at several levels. Why would the Lukan author pass up an opportunity to honour the Twelve at such a memorial supper with Jesus, if indeed he believed the Twelve to be the exclusive participants? The 12 disciples play a vital symbolic and theological role elsewhere in Luke. To leave them unidentified as such at the last Passover meal with Jesus is baffling, unless the intent is to signal a larger group of participants. There is good reason to suspect as much.

In the discussion following the meal about the hard times to follow, Jesus reminds the group around him of his earlier instruction for mission: 'When I sent you out without a purse, bag, or sandals, did you lack anything?' (22.35). Purse, bag and sandals are a clear echo of the instructions to the seventy [-two], not to the Twelve (10.4; cf. 9.3).

If a large group of both women and men followed Jesus from Galilee, it seems unlikely that he would leave them to fend for themselves in Jerusalem while he ate the Passover meal with the 12 men. Passover was a family affair. Jesus would have been the father figure for his new fictive family gathered around the table. But how would so many fit into an upstairs room?

Well, the required room was large. It is called in Greek a *kataluma* (22.11), more an inn than a dining room in a family home. The person who owns, or runs, the *kataluma* shows Jesus' two disciples 'a *large* upper room furnished' (22.12). Such a large room could be expected in a public building, such as an inn. But why the large room if there were only 12 men and Jesus? The upper room of the last Passover supper appears, rather, to be more like the upper room of Acts chapter 1, which accommodated the Eleven along with other men and women for a total of 120 (Acts 1.13-15; cf. 2.1-3).

One of the sticking problems in making the case for a wider circle of disciples in the Lukan presentation of the story of the Last Supper is the term 'apostles': 'When the hour came, [Jesus] took his place at the table, and the apostles with him' (22.14). So accustomed are we to thinking of the apostles as the 12 men whom Jesus chose, that it is difficult to imagine a larger group of trusted witnesses, i.e. 'apostles'. But the seventy [-two] were 'sent' to heal and to preach the kingdom of God. In that sense the seventy [-two] disciples became 'apostles' (sent ones). The number of apostles at table with Jesus is not specified in Luke, leaving open the probability that the 'large upper room' was for a large number of disciples/apostles to whom Jesus entrusted the Eucharistic words, 'including the women who had followed him from Galilee' (Luke 23.49, 55; 24.10). That Luke-Acts views the women who came with Jesus from Galilee as apostolic witnesses along with the men is confirmed by the reference in Paul's speech at Antioch of Pisidia. He says, 'for many days [the resurrected Jesus] appeared to those who came up with him from Galilee to Jerusalem, and they are now his witnesses to the people' (Acts 13.31). The Lukan Paul does not exclude the women from the group of post-resurrection witnesses. Why would the Lukan Jesus exclude them from the last Passover meal with him? In Luke he does not.

Equalizing promise of the outpoured Spirit

Twenty-five years ago today, 14 February 1981, a group of Canadian women called a conference that led to the creation of Section 28 of the Canadian Charter of Rights and Freedoms, guaranteeing all its provisions 'equally to male and female persons'. About two thousand years before that, the Apostle Peter in Acts 2 preached a sermon on the day of Pentecost that promised women and men, slaves and freeborn, equal status under the law of the outpoured Spirit of God. Malestream commentaries to this day make only passing mention of the deep significance of this feature in Peter's inaugural speech that introduces the missionary movement narrated in the Acts. For example, in his massive commentary of some 874 pages on the book of Acts, Ben Witherington III devotes only one tiny paragraph on page 140 to this groundbreaking text, without making any mention whatever of the fact that gender and social categories occupy that text. Those social and ideological features are much more than incidental details. They signal an overturn of accepted socio-religious ideology, which should not be minimized in favour of broad nomenclature such as 'eschatological age' or 'dispensation of the Spirit'. It is time now to examine that electrifying text, Acts 2.14-40.

The setting for Peter's speech to the crowd in Jerusalem is the Jewish festival of Pentecost. When the day had come, the Spirit descended like a rushing wind and filled the house where the disciples were gathered. 'All of them were filled with the Holy Spirit and began to speak in other languages, as the Spirit gave them ability' (2.4) – all of them without discrimination. And the mixed crowd of observers were utterly amazed at how these Galileans could speak the various languages represented among the pilgrims to the festival. One explanation the people advanced was that the Galilean disciples of Jesus were 'filled with new wine' (2.13). This then triggers Peter's expository sermon based on a prophecy of Joel, supplemented by other texts from the Scriptures.

The selected text is from Joel 2.28-32 (LXX 3.1-5). As usual, the source version is the Septuagint. But the Acts redactor (in the persona of Peter) alters the text of Joel in keeping with his understanding of the significance of the event of the outpouring of the Spirit. A comparison of the source text with the Acts rendition of it will help visualize the alterations. Underlined words in both the Joel and the Acts columns indicate alteration in Acts of words in Joel. Bold words in the Acts column indicate words added to the Joel prophecy. The italicized words at the end of the Joel column indicate the closing of the previous thought, which Acts omits.

Joel 2.28-32a (LXX 3.1-5)	Acts 2.17-21
And it shall come to pass underlined{afterward}, that I will pour out my Spirit upon all flesh; and your sons and your daughters shall prophesy, and your underlined{old} men shall dream dreams, and your underlined{young} men shall see visions. And on male slaves and on female slaves in those days will I pour out my Spirit. And I will show wonders in heaven, and upon the earth, blood, and fire, and vapour of smoke. The sun shall be turned into darkness, and the moon into blood, before the great and glorious day of the Lord comes. And it shall come to pass that whosoever shall call on the name of the Lord shall be saved: *for on Mount Zion and in Jerusalem shall the saved one be as the Lord has said, and they that have good news preached to them, whom the Lord has called.*	In the underlined{last days} it will be, **God declares**, that I will pour out my Spirit upon all flesh, and your sons and your daughters shall prophesy, and your underlined{young} men shall see visions, and your underlined{old} men shall dream dreams. Even upon **my** male slaves and **my** female slaves in those days I will pour out my Spirit; **and they shall prophesy**. And I will show portents in the heaven **above** and **signs** on the earth **below**, blood, and fire, and smoky mist. The sun shall be turned to darkness and the moon to blood, before the coming of the Lord's great and glorious day. Then everyone who calls on the name of the Lord shall be saved.

Figure 8.1

Some changes are perhaps for literary smoothness, or for more specificity. The switch of 'old men, young men' to 'young men, old men' (v. 17) may mean nothing more than chronological sensitivity: young first then old. 'Above', 'signs' and 'below' may be added for the sake of specificity. The other changes are more in keeping with the thrust of Luke-Acts. 'God declares' (v. 17) makes more deliberate the divine source of the prophecy now fulfilled in the community of the outpoured Spirit. 'Last days', more so than 'afterward', signals the eschatological character of the outpouring event in the life of the post-Easter community.

Most striking of all is the insertion of the possessive pronoun 'my' twice, with 'male slaves' and 'female slaves'. The implication is telling. No longer are they slaves according to the social convention of the day, obeying their earthly owners. They are slaves under the rule of God, obeying God's will in the social setting. Both female and male disciples receive the outpoured Spirit equally, which means both are equally empowered for prophetic witness (see Acts 1.8).

Finally, the Acts addition of the phrase 'and they shall prophesy' leaves no room for privileging one member over another, one gender over another. Both the 'sons' and the 'daughters' shall prophesy. That is, both genders in the community of the outpoured Spirit will be engaged in bringing the reign of God in the Lord Jesus to bear on the situations of life in which they are involved.

As in other ancient public speeches, someone from the audience can interrupt the speaker; so also here at verse 37. They ask Peter what they should do. His response echoes the prophetic words of John the Baptist in Luke, qualified by the extravagant infusion of the Holy Spirit in the name of Jesus Christ: 'Repent, and be baptized every one of you in the name of Jesus Christ so that your sins may be forgiven; and you will receive the gift of the Holy Spirit. For the promise is for you, for your children, and for all who are far away, everyone whom the Lord our God calls to him' (vv. 38-9). While the setting of the sermon is Jerusalem and the narrative audience Jewish, the scope of the appeal goes beyond Judaeans to 'all who are far away'. Gentiles as well as Judaeans fall implicitly under the encompassing phrase 'all flesh'. The promise of salvation extends to 'everyone who calls on the name of the Lord' (v. 21).

Overall, Peter's sermon carries the promise of salvation prophetically proclaimed, universally applied, and equally appropriated. Rather peculiar is the fact that while Peter's speech in Acts 2 champions the equal giftedness of female and male persons for prophetic ministry in the Spirit of Jesus Christ, there is no prophetic utterance by a woman in the rest of Acts. Philip's four unmarried daughters are acknowledged in passing as having the gift of prophecy, but they do not speak (21.9). Certain women do figure prominently in the missionary endeavours, but their significance is narrated while they themselves speak little or not at all.

Prominent women

Elizabeth and Mary: founding mothers

A number of women figure prominently in Luke, as also in Acts. Two of them stand at the head of the group as founding figures of the messianic community focused in Jesus of Galilee and culminating with the ministry of Paul in Rome. They are Elizabeth, mother of John the Baptizer, and her relative Mary, mother of Jesus (1.5-57; 2.1-7). Both women find favour with God.

Elizabeth was old and barren, a shameful condition for a woman of the time (1.25). God looks with favour on that which the culture sees as shame. The same was true for Sarah, mother of Isaac, and for Hannah, mother of Samuel in the Old Testament. Echoes of those women come through here. The angel Gabriel visits Elizabeth's husband Zechariah in the Temple to announce that his wife will bear a prophet-son. Elizabeth conceives. Her shame is removed. Her son is born to prepare the way of the Lord.

But Elizabeth in Luke is not just a female vessel in the hands of God for bearing a male prophet. She is herself a prophet, being filled with the Spirit, and speaks as a prophet in response to the grace of God. Upon hearing Mary's greeting to her, 'Elizabeth was filled with the Holy Spirit and exclaimed with a loud cry, "Blessed are you among women and blessed is the fruit of your womb. And why has this happened to me, that the mother of my Lord comes to me? For as soon as I heard the sound of your greeting, the child in my womb leaped for joy. And blessed is she who believed that there would be a fulfilment of what was spoken to her by the Lord"' (1.41-5).

Nowhere else in Luke or Acts are women given voice to the extent that they are in the introduction to this Gospel. Elizabeth is truly prophetic in her speech, and completely faithful to the word of the Lord. Her husband Zechariah, on the other hand, because he disbelieved Gabriel's words, loses his power to speak for a time till his son John is born (1.20, 64).

What is so for Elizabeth in the story is abundantly so for Mary her relative. Mary is not barren, but she is a virgin. God's messenger announces to her that she will conceive by the overshadowing power of the Holy Spirit and she will bear a son and call him Jesus (saviour). Ironically, Mary's conception outside of marriage would bring cultural shame upon her, but not so in the wisdom of God. Her son 'will reign over the house of Jacob for ever, and of his kingdom there will be no end' (1.33).

But Mary is not merely a passive female recipient of the grace of God. She, like Elizabeth, bursts forth into prophetic oracle, provocative and promising (1.46-55). Her prophecy enunciates major themes woven into the tapestry of Luke and Acts: God favours the lowly (1.48); shows mercy (1.50); brings down the powerful (1.52); fills the hungry (1.53); sends the rich away empty (1.53); helps/saves Israel (1.47, 54-5).

These two founding mothers exemplify the equalizing grace of God to female servants; they proclaim the word of prophecy equal to their male counterparts in the story, Zechariah (1.67-79) and Simeon (2.28-33). Nor are Elizabeth and Mary the only female prophets in the complex introduction to Luke. Anna is explicitly called 'a prophet', spending her days in the Temple worshipping God with fasting and prayer (2.36-8). Even though she does not speak in the narrative, the description of Anna's prophetic character puts her on a par with Simeon (2.25-8).

Except for one brief mention in Luke 8.19-21 (following Mark) about Jesus' mother and brothers wanting to see Jesus, Mary is not mentioned again until Acts 1.14. She is not listed by name among 'the women who had followed him from Galilee' (Luke 23.49), nor is she named as one of the group of women to announce the resurrection of Jesus to the apostles (24.10). But then, out of the blue, she appears by name in the introduction to Acts. She is not nearly as prominent in the Acts introduction, but she is the only one of the believing women in Jerusalem named as 'constantly devoting themselves to prayer' (Acts 1.14). Her presence at the beginning of Jesus' life, and at the beginning of the Church's life should probably not go unnoticed. Whether the mother of Jesus symbolizes the Church of Jesus Christ is debatable. The notion is far from explicit in Luke-Acts.

Mary the Magdalene (Luke 8.1-3; 24.10)

Another Mary enters the Lukan scenario on two significant occasions. She is distinguished from other women of the same name by her geographical location: she is from a village called Magdala. Hence she should be known as Mary the Magdalene, rather than Mary Magdalene – as though Magdalene were her second given name.

The writer of Luke identifies this Mary by name in two different settings, once in Galilee among the disciples of Jesus, and once in Jerusalem as bearing witness to the apostles about the resurrection of Jesus. Mark and Matthew refer to Mary the Magdalene by name three times, but always in the setting of the crucifixion and resurrection of Jesus in Jerusalem. Mark does intimate that Mary along with other women had followed Jesus in Galilee and ministered to him. Consistently in all three Synoptic Gospels, this Mary is prominent by her first position on lists of women witnesses. The Gospel of John spells out her prominence in the resurrection narrative: Mary, all by herself, is the first one to witness the resurrected Jesus. She speaks to him and he to her in that moving scene. Meanwhile, Peter and the Beloved Disciple had gone home from the empty tomb without encountering the figure of the resurrected Jesus (John 20.1-18).

Returning to Luke, of Mary it is said also that seven demons had gone out (Luke 8.2b; cf. Mark 16.9). Whatever they were, her demons doubtless tormented her. Her deliverance would have brought with it great devotion to the one responsible for her freedom, namely Jesus. Yet this woman devotee – unlike her role in John – does not speak in her own voice in Luke: only through the narrator.

Later malestream interpreters painted Mary the Magdalene onto a very different canvas. She was connected, without warrant, to the female 'sinner' (viz. prostitute) who anointed Jesus' feet in the house of Simon the Pharisee (Luke 7.36-48; cf. John 11.2). But there is nothing in Luke to support the conflation of the two women under the one name, Mary the Magdalene. Seven demons do not of necessity make a woman a whore.

Martha and Mary (Luke 10.38-42)

Because these two women are sisters, and appear in the same pericope in some tension with each other, we treat them together. Martha seems to be the owner of the house to which she invites Jesus. How the house became hers is anyone's guess. It may have belonged to the family and fallen to the two sisters after the death of all the other family members. Of the two women in the story, Martha is the only one to speak, not as disciple-witness but as petitioner to Jesus: 'Lord, do you not care that my sister has left me to do all the work by myself? Tell her then to help me' (v. 40b). The response of the Lukan Jesus is unsympathetic. Martha's work in preparing a meal for her guest is dismissed as too much, too distracting. 'There is need of only one thing', he tells her, and thus denies her complaint and petition (v. 42).

Martha's character in the Fourth Gospel, by contrast, is one of strong faith in Jesus, coupled with a depth of understanding of theological matters. With respect to her dead brother, she believes God will give Jesus whatever he asks. Martha in John is the one to summon Mary to come to Jesus (John 11.17-37).

In Luke, on the other hand, Mary rather than Martha is praised for her part in the hospitality scene. She 'sat at the Lord's feet and listened to what he was saying' (v. 39). It is said that Martha's annoyance at her sister is more about the role Mary adopted, which is not rightly hers in that society, than about her unwillingness to help with the meal. 'By sitting and listening to the teacher, Mary was acting like a male!' (Malina and Rohrbaugh, 1992, p. 348). But the Lukan Jesus legitimates her role as disciple, regardless of gender conventions of the day. Mary is learning the thought and life of the Lord, without which she cannot become a witness to him. That female praxis is the better part, as far as the Lukan Jesus is concerned.

While a number of women come to the fore in Acts, and deserve attention, I will limit the discussion to two prominent women in relation to Paul and his mission among Gentiles, Lydia and Priscilla.

Lydia (Acts 16.13-15, 40)

Lydia belonged to what might be called a women's synagogue. She and other women in the Roman colony of Philippi were meeting beside the river at 'a place of prayer' on the Sabbath day. Paul comes upon them, sits down and speaks to the women. They all listen to Paul, but Lydia comes into sharp focus. The description of her character is colourful. She is a 'worshipper of God', presumably a Greek woman who has committed herself to Jewish monotheism and worship. She comes from Thyatira – in a region previously called Lydia. She deals in purple cloth. She owns a house that accommodates others along with her. The Lord opened her heart to listen to Paul talk about Jesus Messiah, which leads her and her household to submit to baptism.

In uncharacteristic fashion for women in Acts, Lydia speaks on her own behalf: 'If you have judged me to be faithful to the Lord, come and stay at my home' (16.15). In several respects Lydia combines in her person the best of Martha and Mary from Luke. She listens to Paul, a pattern of discipleship like that of Mary, and she invites Paul and his companions into her home as Martha had done for Jesus.

The social and cultural texture of Lydia's character as presented in Acts 16 invites enquiry beyond what is possible here. Some questions arising out of the text must suffice. As a dealer in purple cloth, with a household of servants, was Lydia a rich woman? Was her clientele the nobility who favoured purple cloth? Why did she put forward her faithfulness to the Lord as ground for her invitation to Paul to accept hospitality in her home? Is it possible that she used her income to offer hospitality to people like Paul?

Enlightening as answers to these questions might be, more important is Lydia's place in the literary structure of the text, located socially and politically in Philippi. The figure of Lydia brackets the whole pericope, and stands in counterbalance to the male jailer in the subsequent part of the pericope, who likewise received Paul's message of salvation and was baptized with his whole household (16.23-34). If anything, Lydia's literary place takes precedence over that of the newly converted jailer. 'After leaving the prison [Paul and Silas] went to Lydia's home, and when they had seen and encouraged the brothers and sisters there, they departed' (16.40). Accordingly, Lydia had created a house church in her home, a church made up of brothers and sisters of whom, by inference, Lydia was the 'faithful' listener-leader.

The prominence of women in the early community of Christ at Philippi is born out in Paul's letter to that destination. While Lydia herself is not mentioned in the letter, Euodia and Syntyche are. Of these two women Paul says: 'They have struggled beside me in the work of the gospel … [as] co-workers, whose names are in the book of life' (Phil. 4.2-3).

Priscilla (Acts 18.2-3, 18, 24-8)

Priscilla never appears without her husband, Aquila, neither in Acts nor in the Letters of Paul. Paul met up with the couple in Corinth, stayed with them, shared both their faith and their trade of tentmaking, and then travelled with them as far as Ephesus. More importantly, the couple participated with Paul in his missionary activity. Paul's greeting in his letter to the Romans is very telling: 'Greet Prisca [form of Priscilla] and Aquila, who work with me in Christ Jesus, and who risked their necks for my life, to whom not only I give thanks, but also all the churches of the Gentiles' (Rom. 16.3-4). And Acts bears out Paul's testimony to their diligent missionary work. They even have a church that meets in their house (1 Cor. 16.19). In Acts 18, when this couple listened to Apollos speak at Ephesus, they found his teaching somewhat lacking. They took him aside 'and explained the Way of God to him more accurately' (18.26). Corrective instruction is also missionary work: witness Paul's corrective missionary letters.

What is particularly noteworthy is the joint effort of the missionary couple. At no point, either in Acts or in Paul's letters, does one of them

operate independently of the other. Both are tentmakers. Both correct
Apollos. Both offer their home for church gatherings. Both work with
Paul in Christ Jesus. Both risk their necks for him. Yet one feature of
their joint presence in the texture of Acts 18 stands out: the woman,
Priscilla, is in first position in the presentation of their names. This is
unusual for the time, or even in the present time. (We still receive
some mail in our home addressed to Mr and Mrs, never Mrs and Mr
…). One plausible reason for putting Priscilla's name ahead of her
husband's could be in recognition of her leadership quality and practice.
Of the two Priscilla may have been the one to initiate action, or to
present the Christian message in public. It is not everyone's gift, whether
female or male, to take a leadership role. Where a woman like Priscilla
is gifted, competent and willing to do so, then let the woman lead.

Further reading

Specific topics in the chapter are expanded in the following: Rosalie
Ryan, 'The women from Galilee and discipleship in Luke' (1985),
56–9; Jeffrey L. Staley, 'Changing woman: postcolonial reflections on
Acts 16.6-40' (1999), 113–35; Francis X. Malinowski, 'The brave
women of Philippi', (1985), 60–3; Quentin Quesnell, 'The women at
Luke's Supper' (1983), 59–79; Amy-Jill Levine (ed.), *A Feminist
Companion to Luke* (2002); D. Schaps, 'The women least mentioned:
etiquette and women's names' (1977), 323–30; W. D. Thomas, 'The
place of women in the church at Philippi' (1971–2), 117–20; Beverly
Roberts Gaventa, *The Acts of the Apostles* (2003), pp. 76–81, 236–9,
255–65; Elizabeth Schüssler Fiorenza, *Rhetoric and Ethic* (1999), pp.
1–14, 31–55, 149–73; also *Discipleship of Equals* (1993). Some recent
traditional commentaries and monographs provide insightful context:
Ben Witherington III, *The Acts of the Apostles* (1998), pp. 491–5,
562–9; also *Women and the Genesis of Christianity* (1990); Bruce J.
Malina and Richard L. Rohrbaugh, *Social Science Commentary* (1992),
pp. 283–97; Joel B. Green, *The Gospel of Luke* (1997), pp. 47–107,
316–21, 838–40.

Review questions

1. How does a hermeneutics of suspicion and the practice of deconstruction fit with a feminist practice of interpretation?
2. Why is it unlikely that the implied author of Luke-Acts would be
   arguing for the full emancipation of women?

3. In what respects is the narrative argument of Luke-Acts holding out a promise of gender equality in the community of Jesus Christ? Illustrate from the introduction to Luke and from Peter's speech in Acts 2.
4. Did Jesus have women disciples? Explain.
5. Who attended the Lukan Last Supper with Jesus?
6. To what extent is Luke-Acts suggesting prophetic women leaders for the community of Jesus Christ? Illustrate with reference to Mary the mother of Jesus, Priscilla and Lydia.

9

Theological interchange: 'saying to one another'

The phrase, 'saying to one another', comes from three selected texts in Luke-Acts, the sense and significance of which I take as key to theological interpretation. The texts are: (1) Luke 2.15: 'When the angels had left them and gone into heaven, the shepherds were *saying to one another*, "Let us go now to Bethlehem and see this thing that has taken place, which the Lord has made known to us"'; (2) Luke 4.36: when Jesus cast out an unclean demon in the synagogue at Capernaum, 'they were all amazed and kept *saying to one another*, "What kind of **utterance** is this?"'; (3) Acts 2.12: when people heard the disciples speak in their own language, 'All were amazed and perplexed, *saying to one another*, "What does this **mean**?"' These three texts will come under scrutiny momentarily. In the meantime, something should be said about a theological interpretation.

What is theological interpretation?

Theological understanding comes in several forms in our time and culture. A systematic theologian examines texts of Scripture in search of their meaning, views the meaning in light of the history of interpretation, and then draws up a body of written statements that purports to represent the essence of the themes. The result in effect is a system of doctrine, which is then adopted by faith communities that feel akin to the particular body of doctrine. This may be called *determinate* theological interpretation.

Along the same lines as systematic theology– although its practitioners might claim otherwise – biblical theology summarizes the meaning of the individual books, or groups of books, of the Bible. Librarians might catalogue under 'biblical theology' such titles as 'Lukan theology', or 'Pauline theology' or 'New Testament theology'.

The approach is still a determinate theological interpretation: the interpreter claims to find the meaning resident within the biblical texts. The resultant summary statements become a fixed reference for defining communities of faith.

At the opposite end of this theological approach is an *anti-determinate* interpretation. As the term implies, an anti-determinate approach deconstructs fixed statements, opening them up to *other* possibilities. This model of theological interpretation is characteristically suspicious of stable language. Fixing language forms is a human endeavour that seeks to control meaning, and by extension the people who adopt the meaning as their own.

Stephen E. Fowl, in his *Engaging Scripture*, takes a middle ground between determinate and anti-determinate interpretations. His approach he calls *underdetermined* interpretation. An underdetermined interpretation is less concerned with meaning in texts, and more with the aims, interests and practices that operate in the thought and life of the interpreters. At the heart of this approach is community, and conversation within community. However, the interpreting community is not merely a gathering of disparate people, but a vigilant community and virtuous readers whose very existence has been shaped by the Scriptures being interpreted. Thus the theological practice is one of interchange, of conversation, of 'saying to one another'.

This approach takes the text and its context seriously and critically into account. But it also takes the living, culturally conscious communities into account at the same time. Consequently, theological interpretation allows convictions, ecclesial practices and social concerns to *shape* the interpretation, and at the same time *be shaped by* the act of interpreting. In this way underdetermined theological interpretation is always open to new insights pertaining to the text on the one hand and to the convictions and concerns of the communities on the other. An underdetermined interpretation is the one adopted in the following discussion of Luke-Acts, in hope that vigilant communities and virtuous reading partners will join in the adventure and expand the horizon.

Saying then seeing

It is time now to pick up on the three texts identified at the head of this chapter, to explore the significance of the italicized phrase, *saying to one another*, and the implication of the word in **bold** type that follows in the respective sentence.

(1) Luke 2.15

This text comes in the middle of the account of the angels' announcement to shepherds living in the fields, watching their flocks by night. The angelic word about the birth of a saviour, called Messiah, the Lord, came to them in the midst of their life situation without any evidence beyond the word itself. The shepherds were terrified, even though the word was 'good news'; terrified because the word brought into their world something with which they were not familiar. It was a word of peace among those whom God favours.

The angelic event stimulated conversation among the shepherd community. They were *saying to one another* something that would bring to light and life in them the glory and favour of God. What the shepherds were saying to one another is noteworthy: 'Let us go and **see**'. Their 'saying' together led to their 'seeing' together. 'Seeing' was and is a striking metaphor for **understanding**. Even the good word of angels calls for understanding. Without a valid understanding there cannot be sound judgement and responsible action. If their shepherd life in the fields around the village of Bethlehem is going to take on the meaning of the angels' 'good news', then the shepherds will have to go and see for themselves. Seeing for understanding brings with it transformation of life and thought. When they had seen for themselves the reality to which the word had pointed them, the shepherds 'made known what they had been told about this child'. They returned to their place in the fields with the sheep, 'glorifying and praising God for all they had heard and seen' (Luke 2.8-20).

This little episode about the angels' word to the shepherds illustrates rather well theological interpretation at work. The shepherds heard the word as a meaningful word, talked about it among themselves, and moved beyond the word to find its meaning for themselves, and among themselves. Theological interpretation is not content to discover meaning in a statement and nail it down for future reference. Theological interpretation, like that of the shepherds, involves conversation in community, resulting in life-transforming action, experience and worship.

(2) Luke 4.36

The setting for this text, with its vigilant community of interpreters, is quite different from the pastoral texture of Luke 2.8-20. The scene in this instance is a worship service in the synagogue at Capernaum. Jesus is present and teaching there. Into the service comes a man with an unclean demon. The man thus possessed is completely out of place in a Jewish worship setting. Jesus speaks a powerful word that restores the man to health and, by implication, to his rightful place within the synagogue community. 'Be silent, and come out of him!' Jesus says.

What is of interest here is the response of the worshippers to the word of Jesus. They were amazed, not so much at the miracle as at the word that Jesus spoke. It was not a highly sophisticated word, laced with oratorical nuance. It was simply a word with power to do good to a tormented human being. And so the gathered listeners 'kept *saying to one another*, "What kind of **utterance** is this?"' 'Utterance' is an NRSV translation of *logos*, which is often translated simply as 'word'. What the people in the synagogue observed was a *word* from Jesus that resulted in cleansing, healing and restoration. The Word of God, whether spoken in the person of Jesus, or written in the text of Scripture, is a word on target, a word that leads to wholeness and life. The congregants at Capernaum were amazed, all right. They had seen God at work by the word of Jesus, not merely in the liturgy of the synagogue service, but in the life of a demented man. And they kept *saying to one another*, 'What kind of word is this?'

Question is very much part of interpretation that leads to understanding and thence to judgement and action. Without appropriate question there can be no real answer. There may be propositions, but not answers that have to do with real life. Vigilant communities, and virtuous readers (or hearers) within them, do well to ask questions about the word. Questions put us on the path to truth. Truth may amaze us, even terrify us, but it will not harm us in the long run. According to Jesus in John, 'the truth will make you free' (John 8.32).

(3) Acts 2.12

Once again, the setting of this text is quite different from either of the other two. It is the day of Pentecost, originally an agricultural festival in which the participants thanked God for the 'first fruits' of harvest (Lev. 23, Exod. 23, 34). But in the context of the opening of Acts, Pentecost is the occasion of the outpouring of the Holy Spirit after the resurrection/ascension of Jesus. The effect of this outpouring was a phenomenon unlike anything witnessed previously.

The gathered community of disciples, most of them from Galilee and probably speaking Aramaic, were speaking to a very mixed crowd of pilgrims in languages the speakers had not learned in the usual way. The good news of Jesus had become translatable. The confusion of Babel (Gen. 11.7-9) was being reversed. The whole scenario was beyond the understanding and imagination of the community of onlookers. And, as in the other two texts, the observers were amazed and perplexed. One vigilant group from among them were '*saying to one another*, "What does this **mean**?"' Another group, less vigilant, sneered at the event, satisfied with their everyday explanation, which was really no good explanation at all: '[The speakers] are filled with new wine', the sneering folk concluded (Acts 2.1-13).

Questions of meaning really do matter. But meaning is not merely an intellectual concern, an explanation that stands to reason. Meaning that really matters is meaning in life, meaning that addresses convictions and practices. The people who had gathered to celebrate Pentecost met up with the Spirit of God coming to them in their own language via the vigilant and virtuous disciples gathered together in prayer and expectation. Theological interpretation is about meaning in the life of communities, meaning that will shape them in their time and place. And their place in turn will shape their interpretation of the word.

Israel and the heritage of salvation

Some interpreters of Luke-Acts have pointed to the theology of this two-part work as 'charismatic'. And indeed it is. The Holy Spirit plays a major role in both volumes, and especially in Acts, so we should expect the work of the Apostles to be charismatic: work exercised out of gifts received by the grace of God through the outpouring of the Spirit of Christ resurrected. But Luke-Acts is the product of variegated theological interpretation. A large part of the theological lining of both volumes is historically configured in the narratives. It awaits the coming together of communities to read its theological texture for their time and place in the world. There is a heritage present in the literary texture of Luke-Acts, a heritage of salvation that calls upon virtuous readers to exploit its resources for good in their world, but especially for good in their faithful communities. The invitation lies before us to engage in this beneficial enterprise of God's design to give life and health and peace to the world. 'God's design' – or purpose – is an important phrase in Luke-Acts, as we have seen. The two books illustrate its outworking in the life and ministry of Jesus and of the Church.

Israel

This word construct plays a vital role in the unfolding drama of Luke-Acts. 'Israel' is a religious designation; it involves a particular worship and cult. 'Israel' is a national people; they are constituted together by a covenant relationship enacted by their God. 'Israel' is historical and theological: its people live in time and place and work their way through situations in life in relation to God. And as far as Luke-Acts is concerned, Israel as a religious, corporate, covenant people is subject to the saving benefits of God represented in Jesus Messiah. Upon closer examination of some texts in Luke and Acts we should be able to discern the heritage of salvation that comes through Israel, and in the process be examined and discerned ourselves.

To begin with, the terms 'Israel' (*Israel*) and 'the Jews' (*hoi Ioudaioi*) are not completely synonymous terms in Luke-Acts. 'Israel' is a singular category: one covenant people without regard to the status or attitude of individual members, or identifiable groups of members. Without this distinction it would be difficult to understand why Luke-Acts holds out so much promise for 'Israel', and narrates so much negative criticism for some Jewish people groups, especially Jewish leaders.

In addition to three (of the four) labelled philosophies of Judaism (Pharisee, Sadducee, Zealot), Luke-Acts has several labels for people groups who would lay claim to belong to 'Israel' by natural descent. One broad label that seems to encompass all particular groups is 'descendants of Israel' (*huioi Israel*, Luke 1.16; Acts 5.21; 7.23, 37; 9.15; 10.36). A somewhat more restrictive term is 'men Israelites' (*andres Israelitai*), used, for example, by Peter in his Pentecost sermon in Jerusalem (Acts 2.22; cf. 3.12; 5.35; 13.16; 21.28). Neither of these two labels specifies cultural or ideological difference among the 'descendants of Israel'. But Acts recognizes such difference. In chapter 6 two groups are identified by two quite specific labels, as we discussed in Chapter 4: *Hebraioi* and *Hellenistai* (6.1). Both groups labelled thus in this text belong to Israel, each one probably speaking a different language, and living within a different worldview. Stephen is doubtless a member of the *Hellenistai*, a persecuted group of Jewish believers in Jesus that did not include the Apostles (so Acts 8.1; cf. 9.29; 11.20). But Stephen is also a member of 'Israel', and stoned to death by his fellow members of 'Israel' for his particular views on the Law and the Temple (Acts 7.17-53).

The more problematic term is 'the Jews'. It is problematic especially for those of us living in the post-Holocaust world, trying to overcome the blight of anti-Semitic racism. But the label is not without its difficulties in Luke-Acts. Its presence is much more prominent in Acts (71 times) than in Luke (5 times), a phenomenon that may say something about the growing tension between the new Christian communities and the Jewish synagogue communities next door. In any case, 'the Jews' probably designates biological descendants of Abraham with allegiance to Jerusalem, the Second Temple, and the Law as understood and practised by the leaders of Jerusalem in Judaea. Perhaps a better label would be 'the Judaeans', people who honour the heritage of post-exilic, Second Temple religion of Israel centred in the area of Judaea (*Ioudaia*).

It is time now to discover the heritage of Israel and the promise of salvation that comes with it in Luke-Acts. Is it the case that Luke-Acts highlights Israel only to show it replaced by another covenant people, namely the Church gathered in the name of Jesus-Messiah-saviour? Does the implied author of Luke-Acts make a connection with the symbols of Israel's faith, only to make the point that the sacraments of the Church have superseded them? That is not at all obvious. Israel has been, and continues to be in Luke-Acts, subject to the salvation of God. This God delivered the people of Israel from slavery in Egypt (Acts 7.9-36). The same God again provides a saviour to Israel in Jesus born of Mary. The Judaean shepherds of Bethlehem received the news from the heavenly messengers about 'a saviour', not for themselves alone, but for 'all the people' (Luke 2.10). This saviour was born, not in some anonymous place in the world, but in the 'city of David', city of Israel's model king. Jesus born in David's place is called 'a Saviour, who is the Messiah, the Lord' (2.11). The word is clear: Israel has a saviour, anointed by God for the saving mission, and honoured with the title 'Lord' (*kyrios*).

But there are many other signs at the beginning of this two-volume composition that point to Israel, not as some dispossessed people with the arrival of Jesus and his community of followers, but as the centre of attention in connection with Jesus and his community. Jesus of Israel 'will reign over the house of Jacob for ever, and of his kingdom there will be no end', says the angel to Mary (Luke 1.33). And in Mary's Magnificat she echoes the theme: '[God] has helped his servant Israel, in remembrance of his mercy, according to the promise he made to our ancestors, to Abraham and to his descendants for ever' (Luke 1.54-5). The same holds for Zechariah's paean of praise to the God of Israel:

> Blessed be the Lord God of Israel, for he has looked favourably on his people and redeemed them. He has raised up a mighty saviour for us in the house of his servant David, as he spoke through the mouth of his holy prophets from of old, that we would be saved from our enemies and from the hand of all who hate us. Thus he has shown the mercy promised to our ancestors, and has remembered his holy covenant, the oath that he swore to our ancestor Abraham, to grant us that we, being rescued from the hands of our enemies, might serve him without fear, in holiness and righteousness before him all our days.

Yet Israel in this new configuration of Jesus and his community cannot be an ethnic people unto itself, redeemed of God. Ethnic Israel of God's purpose is to be a light to the other nations of the world (Gentiles), and will be so in the person of Jesus and the Spirit. Again, Zechariah's song celebrates the thought in his prophecy about John who prepares the way of the Lord: 'to give light to those who sit in darkness and in the shadow of death, to guide our feet into the way of peace' (Luke 1.79). People who sit in darkness and in the shadow of death know no ethnic boundaries.

Simeon elaborates the theme of Israel as 'light to the nations' in his speech on the occasion of Jesus' presentation to the Lord in the Temple. Simeon's words are telling: 'My eyes have seen your salvation, which you have prepared in the presence of all peoples, a light for revelation to the Gentiles and for glory to your people Israel' (Luke 2.30-2). Jesus stands in for God as 'saviour' and for Israel as 'light for revelation to the Gentiles'. It is remarkable that the Gentiles have first position in the sentence, followed by 'glory to your people Israel'. Salvation that comes from God knows no boundaries in the human family. Israel is honoured in the person of Jesus, in God's promises through the prophets kept, and in the light disseminated among 'all peoples', without ethnic Israel's identity being eliminated.

Israel and the Church

Many interpreters have noted already that 'Israel' is not taken over by the Church made up of Jewish and Gentile members, nor is the name 'Israel' applied to the Church by the narrator of Luke-Acts. Some have suggested that the implied author of Luke-Acts used 'Israel' exclusively for the traditional, ethnic people of Israel, and 'Church' for the mixed congregation of both Jewish and Gentile people. But that distinction should not be pressed too far. The saviour of Israel is also the saviour of the Church. In many respects, therefore, Luke-Acts applies to the Church precisely the good news that came first to ethnic Israel, to its shepherds, priests and prophets.

Where did this term 'church' (*ekklēsia*) come from in the first place? For the implied author of Luke-Acts it came not so much from the Greek city politic – although he knows that sense very well (Acts 19.32, 39, 40) – but from his Septuagint. There in the Greek Scriptures the term is used abundantly to identify the 'great congregation' (*ekklēsia*) of Israel gathered to hear the word of the Lord, and to get their orders for living life in the land of promise (e.g. Exod. 12.3-47; 16.1-22; Judg. 21.5; 1 Kgs 8.14; Ezra 10.1; Neh. 13.1-2; Ps. 149.1;

1 Macc. 4.59 among many others). The 'Church' (*ekklēsia*) of the Scriptures is faithful Israel: the people of God listening to God's prophets and to each other. And even though Luke-Acts does not apply the term 'Israel' to the congregations gathered in the name of Jesus the Christ, there can be little doubt that the implied author has in mind the faithful congregation of Israel represented by the same term in the Scriptures. Stephen's allusion to 'the congregation (*ekklēsia*) in the wilderness' in his speech illustrates the point (Acts 7.38).

Moreover, a sharp wedge should not be driven between 'Israel' and 'Church' in reading Luke-Acts. Israel, represented in the Jewish people, are the ones to whom the good news of Jesus first came. Peter preaches to them first in Acts 2, and only later enters into fellowship with Gentiles in Acts 10. In Acts, Paul finds a Jewish synagogue first and preaches the good news of Jesus Messiah there before he goes to the Gentiles. But many in the Jewish audiences of Peter and Paul in Acts do not receive the message. In many instances there is outright opposition, even violent reaction to the Christian proclamation (Acts 8.1; 9.23-4; 13.45). But those who receive the message meet in a 'congregation' (*ekklēsia*) to learn the Way of Jesus the Christ whom God raised from the dead. Salvation comes to those faithful to the message of salvation in Jesus the Christ of God. The unresponsive and unfaithful miss out on the joy of God's salvation, whether they come from the nation of Israel or from the other nations of the world.

What is true for Israel is equally true for the Church gathered in the name of Jesus the Christ. Faithful witness to Jesus as the life-giving saviour of the world is the mark of Christian confession in the Church. Where that witness is lacking in the Church so also is the salvation of God. Salvation means peace, the kind of peace the angel announced to the shepherds in the fields. Saving peace brings to an end the hostility between peoples, which, for Luke-Acts, is the hostility between Jews and Gentiles (cf. Eph. 2.11-20).

Repentance and forgiveness

Unfaithfulness to the covenant relationship with God presented a serious problem to the people of Israel. It meant forfeiting the salvation that God had provided by grace. But there is a remedy for unfaithfulness, whether present in an individual Israelite or in a congregation of Israelites. For Luke-Acts the remedy is repentance, a change of mind and heart, away from disobedience and towards the grace and goodness of God.

For example, in Luke 13, when a group of fellow Jews told Jesus about some Galileans 'whose blood Pilate had mingled with their sacrifices', Jesus said to his Jewish conversation partners: 'Do you think that because these Galileans suffered in this way they were worse sinners than all other Galileans? No, I tell you; but unless you repent, you will all perish as they did' (13.1-5). Similarly, when Peter preached his Pentecost sermon in Jerusalem to his Jewish audience, they ask in response, 'Brothers, what should we do?' Peter answers: 'Repent, and be baptized every one of you in the name of Jesus Christ so that your sins may be forgiven; and you will receive the gift of the Holy Spirit' (Acts 2.38). The principle of repentance in Luke-Acts has to do with a return to faithful witness to the goodness of God in Jesus the saviour. It means transforming wicked thought and practice that oppose God's goodness into that which accepts the grace of God. Most wicked of all, in Luke-Acts, was the act of killing the innocent Jesus (Acts 2.23; 3.15; 5.30; cf. Luke 23.47). Even so, says Peter in his sermon, 'let the entire house of Israel know with certainty that God has made him [Jesus] both Lord and Messiah', and there is a remedy even for this sin: 'Repent' (Acts 2.36-8).

Repentance in Luke-Acts leads to forgiveness. Forgiveness sets the guilty free from the dreadful consequences of their actions, and fosters a right relationship with God. This is nothing less than salvation in Luke-Acts. But such salvation is an ongoing affair within the faithful community of God's people, whether in Israel or in the Church. People find forgiveness in God, and thus practise the same spirit among themselves. What greater sin could there be than the sin of an unforgiving spirit in one who stands forgiven? Such an inherent contradiction would be blasphemous!

Baptism

The rite of baptism in Luke does not carry the same meaning as it does in Acts. Luke limits baptism to the ministry of John. He preached repentance from sins and called his hearers to submit to a rite of purification in the river Jordan. Tax collectors and soldiers submitted to his baptism, along with others from the surrounding areas who considered themselves sinners (Luke 3.11-14). Some Jewish leaders did not consider themselves sinners, and refused to be baptized by John. 'But by refusing to be baptized by him, the Pharisees and the lawyers rejected God's purpose for themselves', according to Luke (7.29-30). Even Jesus allowed himself to be baptized by John. Unlike Matthew, Luke does not explain why Jesus would do such a thing. One might suspect that Jesus simply identified with the salvation of God coming to Israel in the ministry of John. Just as he was circumcised at the beginning of his earthly life, so he was baptized at the beginning of his earthly ministry.

Yet John in Luke does not view his baptism as the final stage of the salvation of God for Israel and the world. 'I baptize you with water', he says to those who thought he might be Messiah, 'but one who is more powerful than I is coming; I am not worthy to untie the thong of his sandals. He will baptize you with the Holy Spirit and fire' (Luke 3.16). Beyond this precursory baptism of John, there is no other in Luke. Jesus does not baptize anyone, neither his disciples nor anyone else in his circle. But Acts knows another baptism beyond that of John, the baptism to which John pointed (Acts 1.5).

'Baptism' (*baptizein*) was a common word for dipping, immersing, as one would immerse one's hands in a basin of water. With this sense of the word in mind, one has the image of the Holy Spirit enveloping the community of believers in Jesus so that they were completely under the influence of the Spirit's power. 'It **filled** the entire house where they were sitting. ... All of them were **filled** with the Holy Spirit' (Acts 2.2-4). From that point onward, the rite of baptism was related, not only to a turning away from sins and towards God, but also to the filling of the Holy Spirit (Acts 2.38). This latter makes the baptism 'Christian'; that is, it identifies the recipient with Messiah (Christ), the agent of God's salvation. In that sense, then, the disciples of John appearing in Acts 19 require a second baptism as they exchange their allegiance from John to Jesus Christ. Paul said to them, '"John baptized with the baptism of repentance, telling the people to believe in the one who was to come after him, that is, in Jesus." On hearing this, they were baptized in the name of the Lord Jesus. When Paul had laid his hands on them, the Holy Spirit came upon them, and they spoke in tongues and prophesied' (19.4-6).

One last point on baptism: The rite of baptism in Acts is associated with joining the new community of believers in Jesus Messiah. Baptism is thus a rite of passage into the new group. 'So those who welcomed [Peter's] message were baptized, and that day about three thousand persons were added' (Acts 2.41). Added meant they met the requirement for membership in the community of Jesus Messiah. They could eat together around the same table, celebrate the Eucharistic meal together, and care for one another in the Spirit of Jesus. Even the Ethiopian treasurer, who came to faith in Jesus on the Gaza road and received baptism at the hand of Phillip, could consider himself a member of the new community of Jesus Messiah as he returned to his country in North Africa. Similarly, the pious Gentile woman, Lydia of

Philippi, received Paul's word and baptism and joined the community of Jesus Messiah. And let's not forget the Roman jailer in the same city who received baptism at the hands of Paul and Silas, and his whole household with him. They all became members of the faithful community bearing witness to Jesus, Saviour, Messiah, Lord.

Paul's loyalty to Israel and to Israel's Messiah

One more question needs to be addressed before moving on to another sub-theme. Did Paul's call and commitment to the Gentile world mission change his self-understanding as a loyal member of Israel? After the turning-point in Acts 15, which opened the door of Israel to Gentiles, Paul came increasingly under fire from the Jewish leaders of Jerusalem concerning his violation of the Law of the covenant of God with Israel. In his several defence speeches in court before the tribunal in Jerusalem he consistently declares himself observant of Jewish law and respectful of Jewish symbols and rituals. He circumcised Timothy out of respect for observant Jewish leaders (Acts 16.1-2). He, and some Gentiles with him, observed the rites of purification and sacrifice in the Temple, making sure 'to observe and guard the law' before the eyes of his critics (Acts 21.24-6). He had his hair cut at the port of Cenchreae before heading off to Jerusalem via Syria, 'for he was under a vow' that devout Israelite males undertook (Acts 18.18).

Paul's defence speeches take up much of the latter part of Acts, chapters 21.17–27.32. In all of them he consistently argues the point that he has been faithful to the Law and to the traditions of Israel. Not once does he deny his loyalty to his Jewish heritage. As he stood on the steps in the presence of the tribune of Jerusalem, Paul spoke in the Hebrew dialect, 'I am a Jew, from Tarsus in Cilicia, but brought up in this city [Jerusalem] at the feet of Gamaliel, educated strictly according to our ancestral law, being zealous for God, just as all of you are today' (Acts 22.3). In his account of his dramatic vision of the risen Jesus in this speech, and of his call to go to the Gentiles, not once does he abandon his opening statement about his education in Jerusalem or his zeal for the God of Israel. He puts himself on the same level with his Jewish audience. For Paul in Acts, membership in the new people of God in the Spirit of the resurrected Jesus did not abrogate his membership in Israel represented in the symbolism of Jerusalem.

What seems evident from this exploration of Israel and the heritage of salvation associated with it in Luke-Acts is that 'Israel' and 'Church' are at least compatible partners, and at best interdependent with one another theologically. Without Israel there cannot be Jesus Messiah whose Spirit fills the Church. The Church belongs to Israel, and Israel to the Church. God's salvation belongs to both. Surely there is a lesson here for vigilant communities and virtuous readers: there is no room for hostility, much less a racist attitude, between ethnic Israel and the Church of Jesus Messiah, no room for triumphalist name-calling on the part of one group or the other. God came to redeem Israel, and with Israel the world of human souls 'who sit in darkness and in the shadow of death' (Luke 1.79).

Table fellowship between Jews and Gentiles

The question of table fellowship between Jewish and Gentile believers in Jesus Messiah was not a trifling matter to the implied author of Luke-Acts. Philip Esler, whose treatment of this subject is exemplary, believes this issue 'towers above all others as significant for the emergence and subsequent sectarian identity of the type of community for whom [the implied author] wrote' (Esler, *Community and Gospel* (1987), p. 1). Its significance is not only sociological, but also theological and ethical. Of course, that conclusion begs the question: Is there evidence of a distinct separation between Jews and Gentiles in the first century on the matter of commensality? Esler has demonstrated beyond dispute that the belief and practice of Jewish separation from Gentiles was widespread. The practice was observed in Diaspora Judaism as in Palestinian Judaism. Jewish identity the world over was marked by the kind of food Jewish people ate, as prescribed by Law (Lev. 11.1-47), and by their separation from people who did not so eat, namely Gentile people (Lev. 17–18).

Among the many sources from the Second Temple period (cited in Esler, but too numerous to cite here), one must suffice to illustrate the Jewish belief about entering into table fellowship with non-Jewish persons: the book of *Jubilees*, a second-century BCE composition.

> And you, my son Jacob, remember my words,
> And observe the commandments of Abraham, your father:
> Separate yourself from the nations,
> And eat not with them:
> And do not according to their works,
> And become not their associate;
> For their works are unclean,

Commensality meant close association, which meant in turn contamination of an otherwise clean eating partner, if the other eating and drinking partner happened to be unclean. From a Jewish perspective of the time, all Gentiles were unclean. They ate food that was declared by Law unclean (Lev. 11). If a member of the separated community – as Judaism considered itself to be – entered into fellowship with an unclean person, that member became unclean and passed the uncleanness on to the separated community, much like the spread of disease from one body to another. People of the first-century Mediterranean world, and Jewish people in particular, believed disease and impurity was passed from body to body. Close association, of which eating and drinking was the most notable, could make the otherwise clean person defiled. Leprosy was a case in point. But on the religious and cultic front the separation was just as imperative within the symbolic universe of faithful Jews. The quotation in *Jubilees* bears this out. Separation was imperative for keeping their identity as a distinct people of God's covenant with Abraham. To violate the separation by eating with people of the nations was to put the salvation of the elect in jeopardy.

With this all-too-brief picture of the issue of separation and purity in Judaism before us, it is time to explore the matter in Luke-Acts. In so doing our goal is to tap into the theological implications of table fellowship involving both Jewish and non-Jewish participants. Did the barrier between the two groups come down quickly and easily by their new commitment to Jesus Messiah? Or is there evidence of a certain tension in the texture of Acts, despite the narrative effort to ameliorate it within the context of Christian community? Does the implied author of Acts have an agenda in place for his community of readers to consider?

No one doubts that Luke-Acts is heavily occupied with meals. Luke has more narrative material about meals than any of the other Gospels. And Jesus is focused in virtually every case, either as participant in a meal, or as the one telling a parable about people eating – or not eating – together. Meal narratives in Luke set the stage for the meal narratives in Acts. In Luke the commensality, by all accounts, is between Jewish people of different social status, not between Jews and Gentiles. The latter situation is reserved for Acts.

Jesus in Luke eats with strictly observant Jews, and also with those of questionable purity. One of the most striking examples of proper and improper commensality occurs at the dinner in Simon the Pharisee's house (Luke 7.36-50). Implicitly the Pharisee ('separated one') issued the invitation to Jesus to eat at his table, believing Jesus to be an observant Jew like himself. Otherwise the invitation would not have gone out. All goes well until a woman appears on the scene behind Jesus. She is not an invited guest, nor did she sit at table with the ritually pure Jews. Instead she took her place behind him, as though in obscurity, and 'began to bathe his feet with her tears and to dry them with her hair. Then she continued kissing his feet and anointing them with the ointment' (Luke 7.36). At that point the woman had violated the social-religious code. She was not only a woman, but also a 'sinner'. The scene sparked a discussion, with Jesus the principal interlocutor, in which the woman was forgiven and the Pharisee judged. Even though the woman was Jewish, she had become unclean and passed it on to Jesus with her tears and her touch. Hence Simon's concern. Her touching Jesus makes him unclean.

I submit that the implied author of Luke-Acts has used this story in Luke as prototypical of the commensality between Jews and Gentiles envisioned for the new community of Jesus Messiah in Acts. Other such stories function similarly in Luke. Chapter 14 is set in the home of a leading Pharisee for the purpose of eating and drinking together on the Sabbath. The setting is thoroughly Jewish, Sabbath-keeping being one of the controversial issues, the other being proper commensality. In that meal setting Jesus challenges the purity regulation related to eating and drinking together. 'When you give a banquet', Jesus says to the Jewish host and guests, 'invite the poor, the crippled, the lame, and the blind' (14.13), all of whom represent the marginalized of society customarily not invited to a dinner in observant Jewish homes. This little scenario is followed immediately by one of the dinner guests offering what appears to be a traditional saying: 'Blessed is anyone who will eat bread in the kingdom of God!' (14.15). No contest from the Lukan Jesus on the saying, except for the implicit question: Who gets to eat bread in the kingdom of God? Are the poor, the crippled, the lame and the blind excluded by virtue of their social lot in life? Jesus answers the implied question in his parable that follows. The symbolic foursome are invited and admitted into the banquet in the vision of Jesus in the parable. And their inclusion could mean the exclusion of the ones with proper standing, if they are not prepared to sit at table with the others (14.16-24). Again, this scenario in Luke 14 points forward to the problem of incorporating Gentiles alongside Jews around the table of fellowship in remembrance of Jesus Messiah.

Acts introduces table fellowship promptly after the outpouring of the Holy Spirit on the believing community in Jerusalem, those baptized in the name of Jesus Messiah. Their common life, which included going daily to the Temple, expressed itself in their common fund, but even more so in their sharing food in each other's homes. 'They kept on committing themselves to the Apostles' teaching and fellowship, to the sharing of meals and the prayers. ... Day by day, with one mind they were in the Temple, and were sharing meals in their homes, partaking of the food with great joy and humbleness of heart' (Acts 2. 42, 46, translation mine).

This description of the primitive life of the new community in the Spirit of Jesus Messiah points the way for communities meeting under the same banner, beginning with the Luke-Acts community that first received this treatise. But the first readers were living near the end of the first century, after the success of Paul's mission to the Gentiles. The question of table fellowship had taken on a different aspect in that setting. Members of the primitive community in Jerusalem were all Jewish. Members of the Luke-Acts community were almost certainly not. The majority may have been Gentiles by that time. If so, then the situation puts the whole idea of Christian commensality on another level. Are Jewish sensibilities about table fellowship challenged to the point of the Jews' self-exclusion from the Eucharistic meal? Such a scenario may not be far off the mark in filling in the gaps on the subject of table fellowship in Luke-Acts.

Peter plays a significant role in Acts in resolving the question of table fellowship in a mixed community of Jewish and Gentile members. As noted earlier, Peter is representative of the Twelve, who are in turn the representative Twelve of Israel. Peter is thoroughly Jewish, and thoroughly Christian. His narrative experience and action should stand as a beacon for Jews on the matter of eating and drinking together with Gentiles in remembrance of Jesus Messiah, especially so if Peter demonstrates the practice himself. And he does in Acts 10.

Peter's vision and ensuing action pictured in Acts 10 serve to address the problem of purity laws arising, as they would, out of the common table of the Lord, where Jews and Gentiles associate with each other around a common cup and bread. The other protagonist in the story of Acts 10 is Cornelius, a Gentile centurion and worshipper of God. An angel appeared to him with the message to send for Peter, who was staying in a Jewish house at Joppa. The messengers from Cornelius set out to bring Peter. Meanwhile, Peter became hungry as he sat on the rooftop. He fell into a trance, and 'saw the heaven opened and something like a large sheet coming down, being lowered to the ground by its four corners. In it were all kinds of four-footed creatures and reptiles and birds of the air.' A voice told him to kill the animals and eat. He protests. 'I have never eaten anything that is profane or unclean.' The voice speaks again. 'What God has made clean you must not call profane.' This happened three times before the sheet was caught up into heaven – or before Peter got the point!

The men from Cornelius arrived, and Peter went down to meet them and give them lodging for the night. Next day Peter went with them to the house of Cornelius in Caesarea. Peter went into the house of

Cornelius, and when he found many assembled there he said, 'You yourselves know that it is unlawful for a Jew to associate with or to visit a Gentile; but God has shown me that I should not call anyone profane or unclean.' So he went in, associated with the assembled Gentiles, and announced to them that 'God shows no partiality'. They received Peter, and he received them, baptizing them in the name of Jesus Messiah. 'Then they invited him to stay for several days' (from Acts 10.1-48).

The issue involved in chapter 10 is one of Jewish purity laws, especially as it pertains to Jews eating together with Gentiles. Food is very much the focus. And this comes through in what follows in chapter 11 when the Judaean Jewish believers criticized Peter: 'Why did you go to uncircumcised men and eat with them?' (11.3). Then Peter recites his vision of the sheet with various kinds of animals, reptiles and birds, and all of them declared clean by the voice in the trance. This episode about Peter and Cornelius could easily have become a talking point among the members of the community of Luke-Acts made up of Jews and Gentiles. And it could just as easily invoke discussion among communities of faith today. What cultic rituals and symbols keep people at odds with each other? What group standards work for and against real community in the name of Jesus Messiah?

What is rather peculiar in Acts is the decision of the Jerusalem conference as recorded in Acts 15. Circumcision seems to have been resolved in the conference, whereas the matter of food was more troublesome. Peter's principle and practice of chapter 10 seems to have all but vanished in chapter 15. James announces a decision, and then writes a letter to the Gentile believers that they should 'abstain from what has been sacrificed to idols and from blood and from what is strangled' (15.29). The decision – quite unlike Paul's understanding of the conference (Gal. 2.10) – seems to be the implied author's way of bridging the gap that had doubtless grown between believing Jews concerned about purity laws and believing Gentiles who have no such concern. The Gentiles will have to yield on matters of food. The issue is table fellowship in remembrance of Jesus Messiah. Can members from the two cultural groups eat at the same table, drink from the same cup, and worship the same Lord?

To close this discussion of table fellowship, we do well to touch on Paul's practice in his mission to Gentiles following the Jerusalem conference of Acts 15. Lydia, the Gentile merchant in Philippi we met earlier, invites Paul and his company to stay in her house. She had received Paul's word and was baptized. But she is a Gentile. Her invitation to Paul to lodge in her home is striking: 'If you have judged me to be faithful to the Lord, come and stay at my home' (16.15).

Faithful in what respect? Does her faithfulness have to do with Jewish food regulations? Does her baptism vouchsafe her faithfulness? By the tone of this invitation Lydia knows that Paul, being Jewish, could have scruples about associating with her and her household. The narrative comment following Lydia's peculiar invitation is also noteworthy. 'She prevailed upon us' (16.15b), as though Paul was hesitant to associate with her in her house.

A similar scenario comes through in the story of the jailer. This man, overjoyed at being saved from his shameful fate, washed Paul's wounds and received his word and baptism. The jailer then 'brought them up into the house and set food before them; and he and his entire household rejoiced that he had become a believer in God' (16.34). The narrative is silent about Paul's response to the jailer's hospitality. Did Paul eat the food set before him? Did the jailer and his household eat at the same table with Paul? Questions of this sort are the stuff of theological interpretation. They have to do with the community living out the gospel of Jesus Messiah in a socio-cultural context.

One final example of Paul's close association with Gentiles in Acts happened at Corinth. Paul had been mistreated by the Jews in the synagogue at Corinth, so he said, 'from now on I will go to the Gentiles'. The very next verse has Paul entering the house of a Gentile man named Titius Justus, a worshipper of God. His house is next door to the synagogue. The text about Corinth goes on to tell about some Jews of Corinth accepting Paul's word and baptism, and with them also non-Jewish Corinthians. Other non-believing Jews brought charges against Paul, saying, 'This man is persuading people to worship God in ways that are contrary to the law' (18.13). Gallio dismissed the charges. One wonders what ways were contrary to the law. If Paul stayed at the house of Titius Justus, and ate at his table, then the custom contrary to the law could well mean the custom related to purity. The code of Leviticus 11 may be in view. For the implied author of Luke-Acts, however, Paul is an example of a Jewish believer in Jesus Messiah who finds a way of associating with Gentiles around a Eucharistic table without becoming impure. The implied readers in the vigilant community of Luke-Acts should pay attention and follow the lead of the great Apostle to the Gentiles. The new community of Jesus Messiah welcomes all members of the human family, joins them together by baptism in his name, and invites them to eat and drink together as a memorial of the one who 'took a loaf of bread, and when he had given thanks, he broke it and gave it to them, saying, "This is my body, which is given for you. Do this in remembrance of me." And he did the same with the cup after supper, saying, "This cup that is poured out for you is the new covenant in my blood"' (Luke 22.19-

20). Theological interpretation will take this Eucharistic saying of Jesus, bring it into the vigilant communities called by his name, and involve the members in *saying to one another* something about its significance in their situations in life.

Further reading

Various aspects of theological interpretation appear in the following: Stephen E. Fowl, *Engaging Scripture* (1998); I. Howard Marshall, '"Israel" and the story of salvation: one theme in two parts', in Moessner (ed.), *Jesus and the Heritage of Israel* (1999), pp. 340–57; Eduard Lohse, *The First Christians* (1983); Roger Stronstad, *The Prophethood of All Believers* (1999); Robert J. Karras, *What are they Saying About Luke and Acts?* (1979); Philip Esler, *Community and Gospel in Luke-Acts* (1987); Robert C. Tannehill, 'The story of Israel within the Lukan narrative', in Moessner (ed.), *Jesus and the Heritage of Israel* (1999), pp. 325–39; Ben Witherington III, 'Lord and Saviour: The Christology of Luke-Acts', in *The Many Faces of Christ* (1998), pp. 153–68; Jacob Jervell, *Luke and the People of God* (1972); Luke Timothy Johnson, *The Gospel of Luke* (1991), pp. 176–84, 207–15; Guy D. Nave Jr, *The Role and Function of Repentance in Luke-Acts* (2002); Hans Conzelmann, *The Theology of St Luke* (1961).

Review questions

1. What is a 'theological interpretation' compared to 'systematic theology' or 'biblical theology'?
2. What is the significance of the phrase, 'saying to one another'?
3. In what ways can the title 'Israel' be understood?
4. How important is 'salvation' to the implied author of Luke-Acts?
5. What is the function of repentance and baptism in Luke-Acts?
6. How would you describe the issues involved in table fellowship in the early Christian community?

Bibliography

Bailey, Randall C. 'The danger in ignoring one's own cultural bias in interpreting the text', in R. S. Sugirtharajah (ed.), *The Postcolonial Bible*. Sheffield: Sheffield Academic, 1998, pp. 66–90.

Bauckham, Richard. 'James and the Jerusalem Church', in Richard Bauckham (ed.), *The Book of Acts in its Palestinian Setting*. Grand Rapids: Eerdmans, 1995, pp. 145–80.

Bird, Phyllis A. 'What makes a feminist reading feminist? A qualified answer', in Susanne Scholz (ed.), *Biblical Studies Alternatively: An Introductory Reader*. Upper Saddle River: Prentice Hall, 2003, pp. 67–72.

Broadbent, Ralph, Ivy George, David Jobling and Luise Schottroff. '"The Postcolonial Bible": four reviews', *Journal for the Study of the New Testament* 74 (1999), pp. 113–21.

Conzelmann, Hans. *The Theology of St Luke*, trans. Geoffrey Buswell. New York: Harper & Row, 1961.

Conzelmann, Hans. *Acts of the Apostles*. Hermeneia, Philadelphia: Fortress, 1987.

Court, John M. *Reading the New Testament*. London: Routledge, 1997.

Dietrich, Walter. *The Bible in a World Context: An Experiment in Contextual Hermeneutics*. Grand Rapids: Eerdmans, 2002.

Dix, Gregory. *Jew and Greek: A Study of the Primitive Church*. London: A&C Black, 1955.

Drane, John. *Introducing the New Testament*. Minneapolis: Fortress, 2001.

Drury, John. *Tradition and Design in Luke's Gospel: A Study in Early Christian Historiography*. Atlanta: John Knox, 1976.

Dube, Musa W. *Postcolonial Feminist Interpretation of the Bible*. St Louis: Chalice, 2000.

Dupont, Dom Jacques. *The Salvation of the Gentiles: Essays on the Acts of the Apostles*. New York: Paulist, 1979 (French edition 1967).

Esler, Philip Francis. *Community and Gospel in Luke-Acts: The Social and Political Motivations of Lukan Theology*. Cambridge: Cambridge University Press, 1987.

Fatum, Lone. 'Gender hermeneutics: The effective history of consciousness and the use of social gender in the Gospels', in Fernando F. Segovia and Mary Ann Tolbert (eds), *Reading From This Place: Social Location and Biblical Interpretation in Global Perspective*. Minneapolis: Fortress, 1995, pp. 157–68.

Fitzmyer, Joseph A. *The Gospel According to Luke (I–IX): Introduction, Translation and Notes*. Garden City: Doubleday, 1981.

Fitzmyer, Joseph A. *The Gospel According to Luke (X–XXIV): Introduction, Translation and Notes*. Garden City: Doubleday, 1985.

Fitzmyer, Joseph A. *The Acts of the Apostles*. New York: Doubleday, 1998.

Fowl, Stephen E. *Engaging Scripture: A Model for Theological Interpretation*. Oxford: Blackwell, 1998.

Freyne, Sean. *Jesus, a Jewish Galilean: A New Reading of the Jesus Story*. London: Continuum, 2004.

Gaventa, Beverly Roberts. *The Acts of the Apostles*. Nashville: Abingdon, 2003.

Gifford, Araolyn De Swarte. 'American women and the Bible: The nature of women as a hermeneutical issue', in Susanne Scholz (ed.), *Biblical Studies Alternatively: An Introductory Reader*. Upper Saddle River: Prentice Hall, 2003, pp. 51–67.

Goulder, Michael D. *Luke: A New Paradigm*, vol. I: *The Argument*. Journal for the Study of the New Testament Supplement Series 20. Sheffield: Sheffield Academic, 1989.

Goulder, Michael D. *Luke: A New Paradigm*, vol. II: *Commentary*. Journal for the Study of the New Testament Supplement Series 20. Sheffield: Sheffield Academic, 1989.

Grant, Robert M. *A Historical Introduction to the New Testament*. New York: Harper & Row, 1963.

Green, Joel B. *The Theology of the Gospel of Luke*. New Testament Theology. New York: Cambridge University Press, 1995.

Green, Joel B. *The Gospel of Luke*. Grand Rapids: Eerdmans, 1997.

Gundry, Robert H. 'Richard A. Horsley's *Hearing the Whole Story*: A critical review of its postcolonial slant', *Journal for the Study of the New Testament* 26.2 (2003), 131–49.

Haenchen, Ernst. *The Acts of the Apostles: A Commentary.* Philadelphia: Westminster, 1971.

Hamm, Dennis. 'The Tamid service in Luke-Acts: The cultic background behind Luke's theology of worship (Luke 1:5-25; 18:9-14; 24:50-53; Acts 3:1; 10:3, 30),' *Catholic Biblical Quarterly* 65 (2003), 214–31.

Hauer, Christian E. and William A. Young. *An Introduction to the Bible: A Journey into Three Worlds,* 6th edn. Upper Saddle River: Pearson, 2005.

Hengel, Martin. *Between Jesus and Paul: Studies in the Earliest History of Christianity.* Minneapolis: Fortress, 1983.

Herzog II, William R. *Parables as Subversive Speech: Jesus as Pedagogue of the Oppressed.* Louisville: Westminster John Knox, 1994.

Horsley, Richard A. 'Submerged biblical histories and imperial biblical studies', in R. S. Sugirtharajah (ed.), *The Postcolonial Bible.* Sheffield: Sheffield Academic, 1998, pp. 152–73.

Hur, Ju. *A Dynamic Reading of the Holy Spirit in Luke-Acts.* Journal for the Study of the New Testament Supplement Series 211. Sheffield: Sheffield Academic, 2001.

Jervell, Jacob. *Luke and the People of God: A New Look at Luke-Acts.* Minneapolis: Augsburg, 1972.

Jervell, Jacob. *The Unknown Paul: Essays on Luke-Acts and Early Christian History.* Minneapolis: Augsburg, 1984.

Johnson, Luke Timothy. *The Gospel of Luke,* ed. Daniel J. Harrington. Sacra Pagina Series 3. Collegeville: Liturgical, 1991.

Juel, Donald. *Luke-Acts: The Promise of History.* Atlanta: John Knox, 1983.

Karras, Robert J. *What are They Saying about Luke and Acts? A Theology of the Faithful God.* New York: Paulist, 1979.

Kilgallen, John J. *A Brief Commentary on the Gospel of Luke.* New York: Paulist, 1988.

Kümmel, Werner Georg. *Introduction to the New Testament,* trans. Howard Clark Kee. Nashville: Abingdon, 1975, pp. 122–88.

Kurz, William S., SJ. *Reading Luke-Acts: Dynamics of Biblical Narrative.* Louisville: Westminster John Knox, 1993.

Lee, Dorothy A. 'Presence or absence? The question of women disciples at the Last Supper', in Susanne Scholz (ed.), *Biblical Studies Alternatively: An Introductory Reader.* Upper Saddle River: Prentice Hall, 2003.

Levine, Amy-Jill (ed.), *A Feminist Companion to Luke.* Feminist Companion to the New Testament and Early Christian Writings. Sheffield: Sheffield Academic, 2002.

Lohse, Eduard. *The First Christians: Their Beginnings, Writings, and Beliefs*, trans. Eugene Boring. Philadelphia: Fortress, 1983.

Longman III, Tremper. *Literary Approaches to Biblical Interpretation*. Foundations of Contemporary Interpretation 3, ed. Moises Silva. Grand Rapids: Zondervan, 1987.

Lüdemann, Gerd. *Early Christianity according to the Traditions in Acts: A Commentary*, trans. John Bowden. Minneapolis: Fortress, 1989.

MacDonald, J. Ian H. 'Alien grace', in V. George Shillington (ed.), *Jesus and His Parables: Interpreting the Parables of Jesus Today*. Edinburgh: T&T Clark, 1998, pp. 35–51.

Maddox, Robert. *The Purpose of Luke-Acts* . Edinburgh: T&T Clark, 1982.

Malina, Bruce J. and Rohrbaugh, Richard L. *Social Science Commentary on the Synoptic Gospels*. Minneapolis: Fortress, 1992.

Malinowski, Francis X. 'The brave women of Philippi', *Biblical Theology Bulletin* 15 (1985), 60–3.

Marshall, I. Howard. *The Acts of the Apostles*. Sheffield: JSOT, 1992.

Marshall, I. Howard. '"Israel" and the story of salvation: One theme in two parts', in David P. Moessner (ed.), *Jesus and the Heritage of Israel: Luke's Narrative Claim upon Israel's Legacy*. Harrisburg: Trinity Press International, 1999, pp. 340–57.

McKenzie, Steven L. and Stephen R. Haynes (eds), *To Each its Own Meaning: An Introduction to Biblical Criticisms and Their Application*. Louisville: Westminster John Knox, 1993.

Menzies, Robert P. *Empowered for Witness: The Spirit in Luke-Acts*. Sheffield: Sheffield Academic, 1991.

Moule, C. F. D. *Christ's Messengers: Studies in The Acts of the Apostles (Part 1)*. London: Lutterworth, 1957.

Moule, C. F. D. *A Chosen Vessel: Studies in the Acts of the Apostles Part 2*. London: Lutterworth, 1961.

Moule, C. F. D. 'The Christology of Acts', in Leander E. Keck and J. Louis Martyn (eds), *Studies in Luke-Acts*. Nashville: Abingdon, 1966, pp. 159–85.

Moyise, Steve. *Introduction to Biblical Studies*. 2nd edn. London: T&T Clark International, 2004.

Munck, Johannes. *The Acts of the Apostles*. The Anchor Bible. Garden City: Doubleday, 1967.

Nave Jr, Guy D. *The Role and Function of Repentance in Luke-Acts*. Academia Biblica 4. Atlanta: Society of Biblical Literature, 2002

Neyrey, Jerome H. (ed.), *The Social World of Luke-Acts: Models for Interpretation*. Peabody: Hendrickson, 1991.

Oduyoye, Mercy Amba. 'Biblical interpretation and the social location of the interpreter: African women's reading of the Bible', in Susanne Scholz (ed.), *Biblical Studies Alternatively: An Introductory Reader*. Upper Saddle River: Prentice Hall, 2003, pp. 30–46.

Prior, Michael. *The Bible and Colonialism: A Moral Critique*. Sheffield: Sheffield Academic, 1997.

Quesnell, Quentin. 'The women at Luke's Supper', in Richard J. Cassidy and Philip J. Scharper (eds), *Political Issues in Luke-Acts*. New York: Orbis, 1983, pp. 59–79.

Richard, Pablo. 'The hermeneutics of liberation: A hermeneutics of the Spirit', in Fernando F. Segovia and Mary Ann Tolbert (eds), *Reading From This Place: Social Location and Biblical Interpretation in Global Perspective*. Minneapolis: Fortress, 1995, pp. 263–80.

Richter Reimer, Ivoni. *Women in the Acts of the Apostles: A Feminist Liberation Perspective*. Minneapolis: Fortress, 1995.

Ringe, S. H. 'Places at the table: feminist and postcolonial biblical interpretation', in R. S. Sugirtharajah (ed.), *The Postcolonial Bible*. Sheffield: Sheffield Academic, 1998, pp. 136–51.

Robbins, Vernon K. *Exploring the Texture of Texts: A Guide to Socio-Rhetorical Interpretation*. Valley Forge: Trinity Press International, 1996.

Robbins, Vernon K. *The Tapestry of Early Christian Discourse: Rhetoric, Society and Ideology*. London: Routledge, 1996.

Rohrbaugh, Richard L. 'A dysfunctional family and its neighbours', in V. George Shillington (ed.), *Jesus and His Parables: Interpreting the Parables of Jesus Today*. Edinburgh: T&T Clark, 1997, pp. 141–64.

Roth, S. John. *The Blind, the Lame and the Poor: Character Types in Luke-Acts*. Journal for the Study of the New Testament Supplement Series 144. Sheffield: Sheffield Academic, 1997.

Ryan, Rosalie. 'The women from Galilee and discipleship in Luke', *Biblical Theology Bulletin* 15 (1985), pp. 56–9.

Schaberg, Jane. 'How Mary Magdalene became a whore', in Susanne Scholz (ed.), *Biblical Studies Alternatively: An Introductory Reader*. Upper Saddle River: Prentice Hall, 2003, pp. 113–21.

Schaps, D. 'The women least mentioned: etiquette and women's names', *Classical Quarterly* 27 (1977), 323–30.

Schellenberg, Ryan. 'The Parable of the Lukan Steward in Lukan Context (Luke 16:1-13)'. A thesis presented to the Mennonite Brethren Biblical Seminary. Fresno, 2005.

Schottroff, Luise. 'Working for liberation: A change of perspective in New Testament scholarship', in Fernando F. Segovia and Mary Ann Tolbert (eds), *Reading From This Place: Social Location and Biblical Interpretation in Global Perspective*. Minneapolis: Fortress, 1995, pp. 183–98.

Schüssler Fiorenza, Elisabeth. *A Discipleship of Equals: A Critical Feminist Ekklesia-logy of Liberation*. New York: Crossroads, 1993.

Schüssler Fiorenza, Elisabeth. *Rhetoric and Ethic: The Politics of Biblical Studies*. Minneapolis: Fortress, 1999.

Schweizer, Eduard. 'Concerning the speeches in Acts', in Leander E. Keck and J. Louis Martyn (eds), *Studies in Luke-Acts*. Nashville: Abingdon, 1966, pp. 208–16.

Segovia, Fernando F. 'Biblical criticism and postcolonial studies: toward a postcolonial optic', in R. S. Sugirtharajah (ed.), *The Postcolonial Bible*. Sheffield: Sheffield Academic, 1998, pp. 49–65.

Shepherd Jr, William H. *The Narrative Function of the Holy Spirit as a Character in Luke-Acts*. Atlanta: Scholars Press, 1994.

Shillington, V. George. *Reading the Sacred Text: An Introduction to Biblical Studies*. London: T&T Clark, 2002.

Shillington, V. George. 'Loved by an Enemy', in *On a Journey with God: You come too …* Winnipeg: Springfield, 2003, pp. 31–9.

Soards, Marion L. *The Speeches in Acts: Their Content, Context, and Concerns*. Louisville: Westminster John Knox, 1994.

Staley, Jeffrey L. 'Changing woman: postcolonial reflections on Acts 16:6-40', *Journal for the Study of the New Testament* 73 (1999), 113–35.

Stronstad, Roger. *The Prophethood of All Believers: A Study in Luke's Charismatic Theology*. Sheffield: Sheffield Academic, 1999.

Sugirtharajah, R. S. *Voices from the Margin: Interpreting the Bible from the Third World*. New York: Orbis, 1995.

Sugirtharajah, R. S. 'Biblical studies after the Empire: from a colonial to a postcolonial mode of interpretation', in R. S. Sugirtharajah (ed.), *The Postcolonial Bible*. Sheffield: Sheffield Academic, 1998, pp. 12–22.

Sugirtharajah, R. S. 'A brief memorandum on postcolonialism and biblical studies', *Journal for the Study of the New Testament* 73 (1999), 3–5.

Sugirtharajah, R. S. *Postcolonial Reconfigurations: An Alternate Way of Reading the Bible and Doing Theology*. St Louis: Chalice, 2003.

Talbert, Charles H. *Literary Patterns, Theological Themes and the Genre of Luke-Acts.* Missoula: Scholars Press, 1974.

Tannehill, Robert C. *The Narrative Unity of Luke-Acts: A Literary Interpretation,* vol. I: *The Gospel of Luke.* Philadelphia: Fortress, 1986.

Tannehill, Robert C. *The Narrative Unity of Luke-Acts: A Literary Interpretation,* vol. II: *The Acts of the Apostles.* Philadelphia: Fortress, 1990.

Tannehill, Robert C. 'The story of Israel within the Lukan narrative', in David P. Moessner (ed.), *Jesus and the Heritage of Israel: Luke's Narrative Claim upon Israel's Legacy.* Harrisburg: Trinity Press International, 1999, pp. 325–39.

Thimmes, Pamela. 'What makes a feminist reading feminist? Another perspective', in Susanne Scholz (ed.), *Biblical Studies Alternatively: An Introductory Reader.* Upper Saddle River: Prentice Hall, 2003, pp. 72–9.

Thomas, W. Derek. 'The place of women in the church at Philippi', *Expository Times* 83 (1971–2), 117–20.

Tiede, David L. *Prophecy and History in Luke-Acts.* Philadelphia: Fortress, 1980.

Tolbert, Mary Ann, 'When resistance becomes repression', in Fernando F. Segovia and Mary Ann Tolbert (eds), *Reading From This Place: Social Location and Biblical Interpretation in Global Perspective.* Minneapolis: Fortress, 1995, pp. 331–46.

Trudinger, Paul. 'Exposing the depth of oppression', in V. George Shillington (ed.), *Jesus and His Parables: Interpreting the Parables of Jesus Today.* Edinburgh: T&T Clark, 1997, pp. 121–37.

Whiston, William. *Josephus: The Complete Works.* Nashville: Thomas Nelson, 2003.

Wielenga, Bastiaan. 'Experiences with a biblical story', in R. S. Sugirtharajah (ed.), *The Postcolonial Bible.* Sheffield: Sheffield Academic, 1998, pp. 189–98.

Wilckens, Ulrich. 'Interpreting Luke-Acts in a period of existentialist theology', in Leander E. Keck and J. Louis Martyn (eds), *Studies in Luke-Acts.* Nashville: Abingdon, 1966, pp. 60–83.

Witherington III, Ben. *Women and the Genesis of Christianity,* ed. by Ann Witherington. Cambridge: Cambridge University Press, 1990.

Witherington III, Ben. 'Lord and Saviour: The Christology of Luke-Acts', in *The Many Faces of the Christ: The Christologies of the New Testament and Beyond.* New York: Crossroad, 1998, pp. 153–68.

Witherington III, Ben. *The Acts of the Apostles: A Socio-Rhetorical Commentary*. Grand Rapids: Eerdmans, 1998.

Woods, Edward J. *The 'Finger of God' and Pneumatology in Luke-Acts*. Journal for the Study of the New Testament Supplement Series 205. Sheffield: Sheffield Academic, 2001.

Index of Biblical References

Index of Subjects